# INTRODUCTION
## TO THE
## POEM

## HAYDEN SERIES IN LITERATURE

Robert W. Boynton, Consulting Editor

# INTRODUCTION
# TO THE
# POEM

*Revised Second Edition*

## ROBERT W. BOYNTON

*Former Principal, Senior High School,*
*and Chairman, English Department*
*Germantown Friends School*

## MAYNARD MACK

*Professor of English*
*Fellow of Davenport College*
*Yale University*

HAYDEN BOOK COMPANY, INC., NEW YORK

# ACKNOWLEDGMENTS

The authors wish to thank the proprietors for permission to quote copyrighted works, as follows:

W. H. AUDEN. "As I Walked Out One Evening," "Musée des Beaux Arts," "In Memory of W. B. Yeats": Copyright 1940 by W. H. Auden. "O Where Are You Going?": Copyright 1934 and renewed 1961, by W. H. Auden. "Something Is Bound to Happen": Copyright 1934 and renewed 1961 by W. H. Auden. These selections are reprinted from *The Collected Poetry of W. H. Auden,* by permission of Random House, Inc.

GEORGE BARKER. "To My Mother": Copyright © 1957, 1962 and 1965 by George Granville Barker. From *Collected Poems 1930 to 1965.* Reprinted by permission of October House Inc. and Faber and Faber Limited.

HILAIRE BELLOC. "Lines for a Christmas Card": Reprinted by permission of A. D. Peters & Co.

JOHN BETJEMAN. "In Westminster Abbey": Reprinted from John Betjeman's *Collected Poems* by permission of John Murray (Publishers) Ltd.

GWENDOLYN BROOKS. "Hunchback Girl: She Thinks of Heaven": From *The World of Gwendolyn Brooks (1971).* Copyright, 1945 by Gwendolyn Brooks Blakely. Reprinted by permission of Harper & Row, Publishers, Inc.

G. K. CHESTERTON. "Lepanto": Reprinted by permission of Dodd, Mead & Company, Inc.

JOHN CIARDI. "Damn Her": From *In the Stoneworks* by John Ciardi. Copyright © 1961 by Rutgers, the State University. "Ecdysiast": From *This Strangest Everything* by John Ciardi. Copyright © 1966 by Rutgers, the State University. These selections are reprinted by permission of the poet.

*ISBN 0-8104-5516-1 (soft-bound edition)*
*0-8104-5517-X (hard-bound edition)*
*Library of Congress Catalog Card Number 72-89018*
*Copyright © 1965, 1973*

1  2  3  4  5  6  7  8  9   PRINTING

73 74 75 76 77 78  YEAR

# PREFACE

This book is an introduction to the art of reading poems.

Its aim is to suggest ways of approaching a poem that will remove the bewilderment and mystery that people feel about poetry. We readily admit that often a poem doesn't make immediate total sense, the way a straightforward paragraph like this one does. But a poem usually makes immediate rhythmic sense if you read it aloud, and the other kind of sense we call "meaning" will come with increasing pleasure if the right approaches are made—if, basically, the right questions are asked. The approach used here clarifies what a poem is and does, and how a good reader reenacts the experience it contains.

Literature does not simply comment on human experience. It is itself an experience—an act by one mind that is reacted in the minds of all who read it well. Poetry is the form of literature that depends most on the rhythms and sounds of normal speech, and on the devices of compression and comparison that enable it, once inside the mind, to thrive there (sometimes explode there) with a power of meaning that can literally make one's day complete or even change one's life completely. In other words, a poem *says* much in little space, but it also *is* much.

The first two sections of the book focus on the essentials of any literary act: a situation or subject, a speaker, an audience, and a particular attitude toward all three expressing itself as tone. These combine to give the dramatic experience that is the poem. The third section deals with the poet's dependence on the normal rhythms and sound patterns of language: how he regularizes and manipulates these is illustrated in some detail. The fourth section spells out the poet's shorthand—the devices of compression that are implicit in all uses of language, but most strikingly in poetry: overstatement, understatement, irony, paradox, metaphor, and the other sorts of comparison and contrast.

The final section is a collection of poems for further reading. Portions of some of these poems are used for study and illustration of particular points made earlier in the book; others are entirely fresh. The poems are arranged chronologically from the sixteenth century to the present, and provide a ground for testing and extending the insights developed earlier in the book.

# CONTENTS

Poets are the athletes of language. What we call poetic skill is the ability to get the most out of certain capacities of language that we all use in less interesting ways—just as athletic skill in boxing, baseball, dancing, swimming, or tennis is the ability to get the most out of certain bodily capacities we all use every day but not so powerfully or so gracefully.

The secret of both kinds of skill, the poet's and the athlete's, is coordination. Many elements must be made to cooperate to a single end. In the poet's case, the elements that must enter into cooperation are (1) the subject, (2) the situation, (3) the patterns of rhythm and sound, and (4) the various verbal patterns and techniques that enable him to evoke a maximum of significance from a minimum of words. We will look at each of these in turn.

# *I*

# *THE POEM*

# *AS SUBJECT*

## The subject of a poem may be anything whatever

The subject matter of poetry is as broad as life itself. It is not chiefly con-
cerned, as some anthologies of the recent past would lead us to suppose,
with moonlight and roses, mother, home, and sweetheart, or the horns of
Elfland faintly blowing. On the contrary, it includes every kind of mood,
problem, and experience that human beings know: terror, hatred, mad-
ness, and despair; love, hope, compassion, joy; birth and death; sex and
marriage; nature and man; youth and age; city, country, animal, machine;
the ugly, the beautiful, the brutal, the tender, the solemn, the gay.

The aspect of gaiety in poetry needs particular emphasis, for too often
people today are unaware that good poetry can laugh—or smile, or
chuckle; and much more poetry of this kind should be published in the
books we read in school. Not because somebody wants to show us that
poetry can be bearable, but because laughter is specifically human and
should play its part in our education. What we laugh at is a sign of what
we are, of the extent to which we are civilized.

Here are a few specimens of laughing poetry, from the guffaw to the
smile, which any civilized person should be able to enjoy. If you enjoy
all of them, you will enjoy this book. If you do not, you need it.

[1]                    *Lines for a Christmas Card*
                       HILAIRE BELLOC (1870–1953)

                       May all my enemies go to hell,
                       Noel, Noel, Noel, Noel.


[2]                    *"This Is the Grave of Mike O'Day"*
                       ANONYMOUS

                    This is the grave of Mike O'Day,
                    Who died maintaining his right of way.
                    His right was clear, his will was strong,
                    But he's just as dead as if he'd been wrong.


[3]                       *Spring in New York*
                       ANONYMOUS

                       Der spring is sprung,
                       Der grass is riz,
                       I wonder where dem boidies is.

                       Der little boids is on der wing—
                       Ain't dat absoid?                          5
                       Der little wings is on der boid!


[4]                          *Epitaph*
                    WRITTEN BY A TWELFTH-GRADE PUPIL

                       Here lies her
                       Gone and departing
                       She failed English grammar
                       And died broken hearting.

[5]            *Epigram*

Engraved on the Collar of a Dog I Gave to
His Royal Highness

ALEXANDER POPE (1688–1744)

I am His Highness' Dog at Kew;
Pray tell me, Sir, whose Dog are you?

[6]            *The Gray Squirrel*

HUMBERT WOLFE (1885–1940)

Like a small gray
coffeepot
sits the squirrel.
He is not

all he should be,            5
kills by dozens
trees, and eats
his red-brown cousins.

The keeper, on the
other hand            10
, who shot him, is
a Christian, and

loves his enemies,
which shows
the squirrel was not            15
one of those.

[ 7 ]                       *On an Ecdysiast*

JOHN CIARDI (1916–     )

She stripped herself of all except pretense.
By nature she and Nature lived to feud
over two words. Her life explains their sense:
*born naked into the world, she left it nude.*


QUESTIONS

1 ★ Why is the title of poem 1 essential? What kinds of lines usually go
on Christmas cards? What attitude are Christians supposed to take
toward their enemies? How can you prove that the poet is not a
grouch but a man with a good sense of humor? What is the effect of
rhyming "hell" with "Noel," and of repeating "Noel" four times?
Would the poem be humorous if "friends" had been used in the place
of "enemies"? Explain.

2 ★ What is the pun that makes poem 2 humorous?

3 ★ In poem 3 what characteristics of the speech of some New Yorkers are
being imitated? Does the humor of the poem come entirely from imi-
tation, or is there another factor involved? (Consider especially what
the author does with two words in line 1 and with an idea in lines
4–6.)

4 ★ What connection is there between the subject of poem 4 and the way
it is written? How does the use of imitative language in this poem
resemble that in poem 3? Which would you call the more clever poem?
Why?

5 ★ In poem 5, to whom is the question in the second line addressed?
What clue tells us it is not addressed to another dog? Then why is
the word "dog" used in line 2? What does it mean as used there? What
comment does it make on courtiers? Use the word "dog" in a sentence
of your own that will show the meaning it has in line 2.

6 ★ In poem 6:
   a. What are shown to be the shortcomings of the gray squirrel?
   b. What are shown to be the shortcomings of the keeper? What is he
      the keeper of? Why does he shoot the squirrel?

   c. Which is regarded in the poem as the less admirable—squirrel or
      keeper? How do you know?

   d. How does a squirrel resemble a coffeepot? What does the compari-
      son tell us about the speaker's attitude toward the squirrel? How
      would our understanding of the attitude be changed if the com-
      parison read: "Like a cocky hoodlum . . ."?

   e. In what sense is the poem humorous? In what sense is it not?

7 * In poem 7:

   a. Look up *ecdysiast* in a dictionary. As a whole, does line 1 tell us
      anything about the "she" of the poem that the word ecdysiast does
      not? If so, what?

   b. "Nature" and "she," the poem tells us, "feud"—disagree—about
      "two words." What are those words? What do they have to do with
      the ecdysiast's profession? Which of the two does "she" favor?
      Which does "Nature" favor? Which do *you* favor? Why? (Does
      a dictionary help in defining the difference for you? Why or why
      not?)

   c. Write a paragraph showing that line 4 is simply a different way of
      making the point that is made by line 1. (What does "all except
      pretense" mean?)

   d. "Born naked into the world" is doubtless meant to remind us of
      the ways of looking at life which we inherit from sources like the
      following: (1) "And they were both naked, the man and his wife,
      and were not ashamed" (Genesis 2:25); "And he said, Naked
      came I out of my mother's womb, and naked shall I return
      thither" (Job 1:21). How do these ways of looking at life differ
      from those implied in "nude"? On what grounds can they be
      associated with *Nature?*

   e. By looking in your dictionary, find out from what language *naked*
      comes, and from what language *nude.* Does this difference in
      linguistic origin contribute at all to the different associations that
      we have with these two words? If so, how?

   f. The form of the poem is that of a verse epitaph—a concise com-
      memorative inscription for a tomb. What specific elements in the
      poem remind you of other such inscriptions that you may have
      seen? In what ways is the association of epitaphs and tombs with
      a stripteaser funny? Why is the title "On an Ecdysiast" funnier
      than "On a Stripteaser"?

## The subject of a poem is not the same thing as its theme

### i

A poem's *subject matter* is whatever the poem talks about. In poem 6, above, the subject includes the habits of the gray squirrel, the act of the keeper in shooting it, and so on. The *theme* of a poem, on the other hand, is its "idea," its *generalized* content, which it is possible to state with various degrees of generality. Thus one could say that the theme of poem 6 is that animals follow the law of the jungle and destroy—but that man is worse because he destroys while pretending to follow a higher law. Or one could say, much more generally, that the theme is the hypocrisy of man.

In poem 7, the *subject matter* has to do with a now-dead stripper who is represented as having had a life-long argument with Nature about nakedness versus nudity. The *theme*, on the other hand, is a point about honesty, and the contamination of honesty by any form of pretense, which the poem *uses* the stripper to convey.

In the following poem, much of the subject matter is declared in the title. Two neighboring New England farmers are out walking along their stone boundary-wall in the spring, each on his own side, and as they go they replace the stones that the "frozen-ground-swell" of winter has dislodged. One of them ventures to suggest that the wall is hardly necessary. The other replies that good fences make good neighbors. The first speaker then asks: Why so—unless you need to wall something out? The second speaker does not answer; he simply repeats what he had said before, "Good fences make good neighbors." This, in brief, is the subject matter of the poem. What is its theme?

[1]                    *Mending Wall*

ROBERT FROST (1874–1963)

Something there is that doesn't love a wall,
That sends the frozen-ground-swell under it,
And spills the upper boulders in the sun;
And makes gaps even two can pass abreast.
The work of hunters is another thing:                          5
I have come after them and made repair
Where they have left not one stone on a stone,

But they would have the rabbit out of hiding,
To please the yelping dogs. The gaps I mean,
No one has seen them made or heard them made, 10
But at spring mending-time we find them there.
I let my neighbor know beyond the hill;
And on a day we meet to walk the line
And set the wall between us once again.
We keep the wall between us as we go. 15
To each the boulders that have fallen to each.
And some are loaves and some so nearly balls
We have to use a spell to make them balance:
"Stay where you are until our backs are turned!"
We wear our fingers rough with handling them. 20
Oh, just another kind of outdoor game,
One on a side. It comes to little more:
There where it is we do not need the wall:
He is all pine and I am apple orchard.
My apple trees will never get across 25
And eat the cones under his pines, I tell him.
He only says, "Good fences make good neighbors."
Spring is the mischief in me, and I wonder
If I could put a notion in his head:
"*Why* do they make good neighbors? Isn't it 30
Where there are cows? But here there are no cows.
Before I built a wall I'd ask to know
What I was walling in or walling out,
And to whom I was like to give offense.
Something there is that doesn't love a wall, 35
That wants it down." I could say "Elves" to him,
But it's not elves exactly, and I'd rather
He said it for himself. I see him there
Bringing a stone grasped firmly by the top
In each hand, like an old-stone savage armed. 40
He moves in darkness as it seems to me,
Not of woods only and the shade of trees.

He will not go behind his father's saying,
And he likes having thought of it so well
He says again, "Good fences make good neighbors."          45

## QUESTIONS

1 ★ How many things or persons are mentioned in the poem that apparently do not love a wall? What would you say the "something" is that is referred to in lines 1 and 35? What is implied about the nature of this "something" by lines 36–37?

2 ★ A current comic saying, with which you are probably familiar, runs, "Don't confuse me with facts; my mind's made up." Does this saying seem to you to be in any way illustrated in the poem? Where? Be specific.

3 ★ What do lines 38–42 tell us about the theme? What is the "darkness" referred to in line 41? Is it a darkness that we are all likely to be surrounded by, sometime? Give an example.

## ii

After each of the following three poems there is a series of questions. The last question in each series will ask you to state the *subject matter* of the poem, and then to put into your own words what the *theme* is.

[2]                      *Cliff Klingenhagen*

EDWIN ARLINGTON ROBINSON (1869–1935)

Cliff Klingenhagen had me in to dine
With him one day; and after soup and meat,
And all the other things there were to eat,
Cliff took two glasses and filled one with wine
And one with wormwood. Then, without a sign          5
For me to choose at all, he took the draught
Of bitterness himself, and lightly quaffed
It off, and said the other one was mine.

And when I asked him what the deuce he meant
By doing that, he only looked at me                    10
And smiled, and said it was a way of his.
And though I know the fellow, I have spent
Long time a-wondering when I shall be
As happy as Cliff Klingenhagen is.

QUESTIONS

1 ★ What is wormwood? In what ways are wine and wormwood different?
What would you say each represents in the poem?

2 ★ How does Cliff Klingenhagen's behavior warrant the use of the word
"happy" in the last line of the poem? What does he do that should
make him happy?

3 ★ What is the subject matter of the poem? What is its theme? Why does
Cliff Klingenhagen's attitude bring happiness?

[3]                          *Bredon Hill*
                    A. E. HOUSMAN (1859–1936)

In summertime on Bredon°
    The bells they sound so clear;
Round both the shires they ring them
    In steeples far and near,
    A happy noise to hear.                             5

Here of a Sunday morning
    My love and I would lie,
And see the colored counties,
    And hear the larks so high
    About us in the sky.                               10

---

°**Bredon:** a British hill overlooking two shires (counties).

The bells would ring to call her
   In valleys miles away:
"Come all to church, good people;
   Good people, come and pray."
   But here my love would stay.        15

And I would turn and answer
   Among the springing thyme,
"Oh, peal upon our wedding,
   And we will hear the chime,
   And come to church in time."      20

But when the snows at Christmas
   On Bredon top were strown,
My love rose up so early
   And stole out unbeknown
   And went to church alone.      25

They tolled the one bell only,
   Groom there was none to see,
The mourners followed after,
   And so to church went she,
   And would not wait for me.      30

The bells they sound on Bredon,
   And still the steeples hum.
"Come all to church, good people,"—
   Oh, noisy bells, be dumb;
   I hear you, I will come.      35

## QUESTIONS

1 ★ What two times of the year are dealt with in the poem? Why is the sound of the bells a "happy noise" in the first stanza? When do the lovers intend to go to church together? Why does the speaker's loved one in fact go alone? What word in line 11 hints that she may be the first to go?

2 ★ What did the speaker think the bells were reminding him of when he lay on Bredon Hill? What does he discover they are also reminding him of by the end of the poem? When he says he will obey the bells (line 35), what does he mean?

3 ★ What is the subject matter of the poem? What is its theme?

[ 4 ] *The Big I*

JOHN HALL WHEELOCK (1886–    )

A bird with a big eye
In at my window poked his head,
And fixed me with a big eye.
"Who are you? What do you want?" I said.
"Me? You mean you don't know me?" he made reply,  5
"Why, I am I. Who are you?"
"I, too, am I," I bashfully admitted.
Now here was a big I-dea to work upon,
For if each one is I, must we not all be one?
Then I am one in all, and all are one in me.  10
I observed, thinking it over carefully,
That I wondered, this being true,
What made us feel so separate, so alone.
"*I* did," shouted the bird,
And I turned to strangle him, but he was flown.  15

QUESTIONS

1 ★ State in your own words the "big I-dea" that is referred to in line 8 and elaborated in lines 9–10. Just how does the experience described in lines 1–7 raise this "I-dea"? What evidence from our normal experience as human beings is brought forward in line 13 to contradict the conclusion in line 10?

2 ★ In lines 6–7, as the two speakers confront each other, both say, "'I am I." Is the conclusion in line 10 the only conclusion that can emerge from this situation? How does the situation prepare the reader for what is said in line 13? in line 15? What does the emphasis on "I" throughout

the poem have to do with line 15? How would you relate this emphasis to the bird's "big eye"?

3 ★ Discuss the merit of each of the following sentences as an interpretation of the poem: (a) The poem is about the paradoxical character of the human ego, which is both selfish and unselfish, and which longs both for individualism and community; (b) The poem is about the difference between philosophy and experience, reason and feeling; (c) The poem is about the human world's irreconcilability with the world of nature represented in the bird.

4 ★ What is the subject matter of the poem? What is its theme?

## The meaning of a poem is not the same thing as its subject or its theme

i

The theme of a poem is part of its meaning, just as is its subject matter. But neither subject matter nor theme nor both together make the whole meaning. The whole meaning of a poem is the whole poem as it stands, and nothing less.

This fact must be stressed because one of the commonest misconceptions of inexperienced readers is that a poem contains a meaning in the same way that a pill bottle contains a pill: you swallow the pill and throw the bottle away. Nothing could be farther from the truth. Good poems are much more like people—or plants—than they are like pill bottles. To be sure, it is often *convenient*, as we have just seen, to talk of the *theme* of a poem and of its *subject* as if these were separable things that the rest of the poem exists only to convey. In the same way, it is *convenient* to talk of a man's or a woman's "character," "temperament," "intelligence." But just as none of these abstract words can substitute for the whole person, who is always flesh, blood, and bone—a person with eyes and hair of a certain color, a brown mole behind the right ear, and a passion for fried parsnips —so no theme or subject can substitute for the whole poem. The whole meaning of a poem such as "The Gray Squirrel," which you have already read, is not simply that squirrels are destructive and that keepers shoot them, nor that human beings are hypocrites who preach one thing and practice another, nor even a combination of these. It is this theme as modified by a great many features of poems that we have so far not mentioned: the poem's speaker, audience, tone, rhythm, meter, and many more. To illustrate specifically, meaning is substantially modified in "The Gray Squirrel" by (among other things) the comparison of squirrel and coffeepot with which the poem opens. This comparison is not only arresting but consciously comic. It begets in us from the very start an amused attitude toward squirrels (rather than, say, a hostile attitude), and it thus persuades us to see the squirrel as something of a charming "oddball," damaging in some respects, no doubt, but harmless to human beings, and surely not a creature to be lightheartedly destroyed.

Consider in this connection two poems that have something in common as to theme, but differ enormously as to subject and even more as to their whole meaning.

[1]              *God's Will for You and Me*
                     ANONYMOUS

           Just to be tender, just to be true,
           Just to be glad the whole day through,
           Just to be merciful, just to be mild,
           Just to be trustful as a child,
           Just to be gentle and kind and sweet,                    5
           Just to be helpful with willing feet,
           Just to be cheery when things go wrong,
           Just to drive sadness away with a song,
           Whether the hour is dark or bright,
           Just to be loyal to God and right,                       10
           Just to believe that God knows best,
           Just in his promises ever to rest—
           Just to let love be our daily key,
           That is God's Will for you and me.

[2]      *A Man Who Had Fallen Among Thieves*°
              E. E. CUMMINGS (1894–1962)

           a man who had fallen among thieves
           lay by the roadside on his back
           dressed in fifteenthrate ideas
           wearing a round jeer for a hat

°**Title:** See Luke 10:30–37.

fate per a somewhat more than less                    5
emancipated evening
had in return for consciousness
endowed him with a changeless grin

whereon a dozen staunch and leal°
citizens did graze at pause                            10
then fired by hypercivic zeal
sought newer pastures or because

swaddled with a frozen brook
of pinkest vomit out of eyes
which noticed nobody he looked                         15
as if he did not care to rise

one hand did nothing on the vest
its wideflung friend clenched weakly dirt
while the mute trouserfly confessed
a button solemnly inert.                               20

Brushing from whom the stiffened puke
i put him all into my arms
and staggered banged with terror through
a million billion trillion stars.

Poem 1 is an uplift poem of the sort that used to be printed on edify-
ing calendars and nailed to the bathroom wall beside the shaving mirror.
The weakness of such poetry is that it falsifies life by making matters that
are very complicated and very difficult appear simple and easy. "Just to
be merciful" is a case in point. The sentiment is noble. But how does one
go about being "merciful" without destroying justice? Or just without
destroying mercy? The question is one of the profoundest puzzles that
every human community—and every classroom—have to face. The poet
shows no awareness of the puzzle. Or consider: "Just to be loyal to God
and right." This is also a noble idea—but in practice it is not always pos-
sible to know whether we *are* right, and it is dangerous to be too sure

°**leal:** loyal.

about it. The men who hanged the "witches" at Salem believed intensely that they were right. So did the slaveholders in both North and South. Most Americans think now that it brought more good than evil to drop the atomic bomb on Hiroshima in 1945. Most Japanese do not agree. Who is right? So here again the poet shows no true understanding of what his own words mean. And because he does not, his *intended* meaning is eventually undermined altogether by his actual *words*. His intended meaning in the poem as a whole might be expressed, "How little God asks of us! Just to be tender . . . ," and so on. But by the time we come to the end of the poem, his words, when we think about them, have departed so far from this intention that they actually appear to be saying, almost with a cynical sneer, "All God asks of us is the impossible. Just to be tender . . ."

Poem 2 is a lot harder to understand at first sight than poem 1, but precisely because it has something to say. It is based, as its title tells us, on the parable of the Good Samaritan, a man of a despised people who gives aid to a traveler "who had fallen among thieves," been stripped of his clothes, and left half dead by the roadside. The story tells us that a priest and a Levite—men of greater respectability and standing in the community—see the wounded man, but they pass by on the other side. But when the Samaritan comes along, he tends the man's wounds, lodges him at an inn, and leaves money with the landlord of the inn for further care after the Samaritan himself has gone. The poem's aim is to make us see and feel this situation afresh—in modern terms, the terms in which we ourselves will meet with it.

The author of poem 2 does not, like the author of poem 1, falsify reality by making what is hard or questionable seem easy and clear. The victim in poem 2, so far as we can tell, is not an outstanding or even an admirable man: he appears to have "fifteenthrate" ideas and an attitude toward society that can be described as "a round jeer." There is certainly no social credit to be gained by rescuing him. Far from it. He has been on a drunken binge (5–6), wears the exasperating silly grin of the dead drunk (8), is half unbuttoned (19–20), shows no interest in being helped (15–16), and probably, thanks to the "pinkest vomit" (14), smells disgusting. Several "staunch and leal" citizens have already looked at him and passed by (9–16). But the speaker of the poem, with a lunge of pity that overcomes his physical revulsion (emphasized in the strong words "stiffened puke") accepts the full nature of mankind with *all* its capacities, both for degradation and for greatness—"i put him all into my arms"—and by doing so finds he has entered a new dimension, even a new world:

> and staggered banged with terror through
> a million billion trillion stars.

QUESTIONS

1 ★ Do you see any other phrases in poem 1 besides the two already singled out that indicate that the poet is falsifying by making what is hard, complex, or impossible sound simple, or what is undesirable sound good? Is cheeriness (line 7), for example, necessarily a desirable reaction when things go wrong?

2 ★ Does poem 1 have any characteristics, in addition to the thoughtlessness of its words, that might be described as childish and silly? What are they?

3 ★ In poem 2, the term "emancipated" is used to describe a drunken binge. Does it seem to you the sort of term that is suited to such use? Could it be an example of one of those "fifteenthrate ideas" by which the victim apparently has directed his life? What was he "emancipated" from?

4 ★ The citizens in poem 2 are said to be "staunch and leal." What are we to suppose they are loyal *to*? They are "fired by hypercivic zeal." Zeal for what?

5 ★ It has been said that poem 2 is about the eternal conflict between the conscience of the individual and the conventions of society. Can you see why? Which side is the poet on? Which side is the New Testament parable on?

6 ★ "Emancipated," as we have seen above, is the kind of word a drunken man might use to conceal from himself the real nature of his alcoholism. "Staunch" and "leal" are old-fashioned words such as the citizens might use to conceal from themselves their real motives for passing by on the other side. What does the poem suggest the real motives are? What are these citizens likened to by the words "graze" in line 10 and "pastures" in line 12?

7 ★ In line 22, the poet makes the speaker speak of himself with a small instead of a capital *I*. Does this small *i* have any significance? In line 23 why do you suppose the speaker describes himself as "banged with terror"?

## ii

Here are four more poems in which subject and theme are clearly modified by each poet's handling.

[3]                    *Delight in Disorder*
                 ROBERT HERRICK (1591–1674)

           A sweet disorder in the dress
           Kindles in clothes a wantonness:
           A lawn° about the shoulders thrown
           Into a fine distraction:
           An erring lace, which here and there                    5
           Enthralls the crimson stomacher:°
           A cuff neglectful, and thereby
           Ribands to flow confusedly:
           A winning wave (deserving note)
           In the tempestuous petticoat:                          10
           A careless shoestring, in whose tie
           I see a wild civility:
           Do more bewitch me, than when art
           Is too precise in every part.


## QUESTIONS

1 ★ What details in lines 3–12 make specific the "sweet disorder" spoken
    of in line 1?

2 ★ Why does the disorder "more bewitch" the speaker than would "art"
    that is "too precise"?

3 ★ What is the subject matter of the poem? What is its theme?

4 ★ Try to indicate as specifically as possible how the choice of words
    qualifies the theme. Consider, for instance, "sweet disorder," "wanton-
    ness," "fine distraction," "erring lace," "winning wave," "tempestuous
    petticoat," and "wild civility." What is the nature of the "delight" that
    the speaker finds in disorder? Is the disorder itself "artful"?

---

°lawn: sheer linen.   °stomacher: the center front section, usually em-
broidered, of the waist of a woman's dress.

[4]              *Bells for John Whiteside's Daughter*

JOHN CROWE RANSOM (1888–    )

There was such speed in her little body,
And such lightness in her footfall,
It is no wonder her brown study
Astonishes us all.

Her wars were bruited in our high window.                    5
We looked among orchard trees and beyond,
Where she took arms against her shadow,
Or harried unto the pond

The lazy geese, like a snow cloud
Dripping their snow on the green grass,                       10
Tricking and stopping, sleepy and proud,
Who cried in goose, Alas,

For the tireless heart within the little
Lady with rod that made them rise
From their noon apple-dreams, and scuttle                    15
Goose-fashion under the skies!

But now go the bells, and we are ready;
In one house we are sternly stopped
To say we are vexed at her brown study,
Lying so primly propped.                                      20

QUESTIONS

1 ★ What does a "brown study" usually mean? What does it mean in this
    case? Why does the girl's stillness seem astonishing?

2 ★ What activities of the young girl does the speaker recall? Why does
    he refer to them as "wars"? In what sense were they "wars"? In what
    sense not?

3 ★ How does the length of the sentence that occupies stanzas two, three,
    and four help convey the "tireless" character of the "little lady with
    rod"? What is the attitude of the geese toward their disturber?

4 ★ "Astonishes" (line 4) and "vexed" (line 19) indicate a response differ-
ent from the one we might ordinarily expect to the death of a young
girl. So does the humorous treatment of the harried geese. So do
phrases like "sternly stopped" and "primly propped." What is the
speaker plainly seeking to avoid in treating the little girl's death?

5 ★ Show how the way the subject matter is handled defines the meaning
of the poem.

[5]        *A Narrow Fellow in the Grass*
            EMILY DICKINSON (1830–1886)

A narrow fellow in the grass
Occasionally rides;
You may have met him,—did you not?
His notice sudden is.

The grass divides as with a comb,                    5
A spotted shaft is seen;
And then it closes at your feet
And opens further on.

He likes a boggy acre,
A floor too cool for corn.                            10
But when a boy, and barefoot,
I more than once at noon

Have passed, I thought, a whiplash
Unbraiding in the sun,—
When, stooping to secure it,                          15
It wrinkled, and was gone.

Several of nature's people
I know, and they know me;
I feel for them a transport
Of cordiality;                                        20

But never met this fellow,
Attended or alone,
Without a tighter breathing,
And zero at the bone.

## QUESTIONS

1 ⋆ What is the subject matter of the poem? Who or what is the "narrow fellow in the grass"? What details of the way he acts identify him?

2 ⋆ Is there anything in the first five stanzas to suggest that the "narrow fellow" would cause the "tighter breathing,/And zero at the bone" mentioned in the last two lines? Consider what is suggested by the use of such terms as "narrow fellow," "comb," "shaft," "whiplash," and "wrinkled"—and such odd syntax as "His notice sudden is." How do these seemingly whimsical descriptive phrases contrast with, and at the same time support, the last two lines to give a special meaning to the encounter?

3 ⋆ What famous encounter in the Bible helps to account for this special meaning?

[ 6 ] *The Sea Turtle and the Shark*

MELVIN B. TOLSON (1900–1966)

Strange but true is the story
of the sea-turtle and the shark—
the instinctive drive of the weak to survive
in the oceanic dark.
Driven,                                              5
riven
by hunger
from abyss to shoal,
sometimes the shark swallows
the sea-turtle whole.                               10
"The sly reptilian marine
withdraws,
into the shell

of his undersea craft,
his leathery head and the rapacious claws                    15
that can rip
a rhinoceros' hide
or strip
a crocodile to fare-thee-well;
now,                                                          20
*inside* the shark,
the sea-turtle begins the churning seesaws
of his descent into pelagic hell;
then . . . *then,*
with ravenous jaws                                           25
that can cut sheet steel scrap,
the sea-turtle gnaws
. . . and gnaws . . . and gnaws . . .
his way in a way that appalls—
*his* way to freedom,                                        30
beyond the vomiting dark,
beyond the stomach walls
of the shark."

## QUESTIONS

1 * The subject matter of this poem is obvious: the shark swallows the
sea-turtle, and the sea-turtle gnaws his way to freedom, destroying
the shark. What causes does the poem assign to the shark's action?
To the sea-turtle's? By what means does the poem communicate the
compelling power of these forces? What does the sea-setting con-
tribute to our sense of their power?

2 * What indications can you discover in the poem that the subject matter
may not be all that the poet is interested in conveying to us—that
the shark's and sea-turtle's blind destruction of each other may
incorporate a theme more immediately relevant to *human* concerns?
Which of the following ways of stating something more is best sup-
ported by the poem's actual details: (1) Our world is a place where
only blind instinctive drives to survive ultimately count; (2) Our world
everywhere presents us with the paradox of the destroyer who is
destroyed by his own rapacity, or by his own arrogant use of power;

(3) The black ghetto, swallowed up in a rapacious white society, will inevitably destroy that society in achieving its freedom. Choose one of these interpretations and defend it in a paragraph or two.

3 * In Shakespeare's *King Lear*, a character sees humanity (as in Tolson's poem) preying on itself "like monsters of the deep"; and Thomas Hobbes, a seventeenth-century philosopher, conceived human society as a "war *of* all *on* all." What are your own views on this matter? Is society simply a polite mask beneath which men prey on each other? or a brotherhood? or something in between? Do *you* behave like the shark and sea-turtle? If yes, what drives you? Hunger? Greed? Cruelty? Stupidity? If no, what prevents you? Fear? Social habit? Natural affection? Religious training? Ability to imagine how another feels? When did you last try to imagine how others feel? What success did you have?

4 * Now that you have considered both subject-matter and theme in Tolson's poem, consider the *particular* shape that it gives these by its formal characteristics. What elements of grim humor may be detected in the word choices generally? in the comparisons in lines 11 and 14? in the parallel established between the situation described in lines 6–7 and that described in lines 27–33? in the exaggeration of lines 25–26? Do rhythm and rhyme achieve any effects that seem appropriate to the story being told? Can you account for the mixture of very short with longer lines? for the rise in intensity of feeling and attitude that seems to take place between line 1 and lines 28–33? Trace the rise in detail.

### iii

Compare the following three poems, whose themes are much alike. Then answer the questions at the end of each.

As you read the following poems, note carefully the ways in which the "meaning" of each is affected by the poet's individual way of handling the common theme.

[ 7 ]                    *Without Benefit of Declaration*
                        LANGSTON HUGHES (1902–1967)

                        Listen here, Joe,
                        Don't you know

That tomorrow
You got to go
Out yonder where                                    5
The steel winds blow?

Listen here, kid,
It's been said
Tomorrow you'll be dead
Out there where                                     10
The snow is lead.
Don't ask me why
Just go ahead and die.

Hidden from the sky
Out yonder you'll lie:                              15
A medal to your family—
In exchange for
A guy.

*Mama, don't cry.*


QUESTIONS

1 * In each of the poem's three stanzas, nature's world is contrasted with man's world as seen in time of war. How and where is this contrast achieved in each case? What is the purpose of it?

2 * The last line is set apart from the body of the poem. Why so? What new perspective on man's world does it bring before us? What sort of comment does this new perspective make on the activities of lines 1–18?

3 * Most of the poem is addressed to a "Joe," who is also a "kid," who does not anywhere make a reply. Does this add to or detract from the poem's effect? Explain.

[ 8 ]                    *Dulce et Decorum Est*°
                    WILFRED OWEN (1893–1918)

Bent double, like old beggars under sacks,
Knock-kneed, coughing like hags, we cursed through sludge,
Till on the haunting flares we turned our backs,
And toward our distant rest began to trudge.
Men marched asleep. Many had lost their boots,                      5
But limped on, blood-shod. All went lame, all blind;
Drunk with fatigue; deaf even to the hoots
Of gas-shells dropping softly behind.

Gas! Gas! Quick, boys!—An ecstasy of fumbling,
Fitting the clumsy helmets just in time,                            10
But someone still was yelling out and stumbling
And floundering like a man in fire or lime.—
Dim through the misty panes and thick green light,
As under a green sea, I saw him drowning.

In all my dreams before my helpless sight                          15
He plunges at me, guttering, choking, drowning.

If in some smothering dreams, you too could pace
Behind the wagon that we flung him in,
And watch the white eyes writhing in his face,
His hanging face, like a devil's sick of sin;                      20
If you could hear, at every jolt, the blood
Come gargling from the froth-corrupted lungs,
Bitter as the cud
Of vile, incurable sores on innocent tongues,—
My friend, you would not tell with such high zest                  25
To children ardent for some desperate glory,
The old Lie: *Dulce et decorum est*
*Pro patria mori.*

---

°**Dulce et decorum est [pro patria mori]:** Sweet and fitting it is to die for
one's country; a quotation from the Roman poet Horace.

QUESTIONS

1 ★ How has the speaker created a sense of utter weariness and despair in the first stanza? What kind of men have these soldiers become?

2 ★ What are the men headed toward when the gas attack occurs? What specifically happens to the one man who cannot get his gas mask on in time? How do lines 13–14 prepare for the "smothering dreams" described in the last stanza?

3 ★ The speaker is not describing something that is happening, but something that has happened. Why does the memory of it haunt him? Why is he telling it? To whom?

4 ★ The subject matter is the memory of the horrible death of one man in war. What is the theme?

5 ★ The speaker argues that the sentiment from Horace is a "Lie." Was there anything to be said on the other side in Horace's day? Is there now? Why or why not?

[ 9 ]                    *plato told him*

E. E. CUMMINGS  (1894–1962)

plato told

him:he couldn't
believe it(jesus

told him;he
wouldn't believe                                    5
it)lao

tsze
certainly told
him,and general
(yes                                               10
mam)
sherman;

and even
(believe it
or                                          15

not)you
told him:i told
him;we told him
(he didn't believe it,no

sir)it took                                  20
a nipponized bit of
the old sixth

avenue
el;in the top of his head:to tell

him                                          25

## QUESTIONS

What Plato, Jesus, Lao-tsze, General Sherman, and "even . . . you . . .
[and] I . . . [and] we told him" was, in General Sherman's words: "War
is hell." (General Sherman made several devastating marches through
parts of the South near the close of the Civil War and was felt by South-
erners to have put his view of war into practice.) The reference in lines
20–25 is to the fact that the Sixth Avenue El (elevated train tracks running
along Sixth Avenue in New York City) was torn down and sold in part to
the Japanese (Nipponese) in the 1930's as scrap metal, which they used to
manufacture armaments.

1 ★ Who is the "him" of lines 2, 4, 9, 17, 18, and 25?

2 ★ What are the nationalities and approximate dates of Plato? Jesus?
   Lao-tsze? What idea would be lost if the three names were all of one
   nationality (for example, Moses, Isaiah, Jesus) or of one period?

3 ★ Why isn't "he" convinced? What does convince him? In what condi-
   tion is he when he at last learns? What does this slowness suggest
   about "his" long-run future?

4 ★ The arrangement of words in the poem seeks to act out the thrust of telling and the counterthrust of not believing. How? What words or phrases are repeated? In what pattern? What marked change in the pattern takes place in lines 20–25 to act out the change that has taken place in "him"? The poem ends with a powerful emphasis on "him," which stands alone in line 25. Can you see why?

5 ★ What is gained by the change from "couldn't" in line 2 to "wouldn't" in line 5? What repetition in lines 16–18 brings to a climax the effort to persuade "him" by reason? What rhyme in line 24 emphasizes the change in pattern mentioned in question 4?

6 ★ How does the intrusion of "yes mam" between "general" and "sherman" suggest surprise that a general would say such a thing? What other intrusions serve the same end? What is the purpose of such intrusions?

7 ★ What is the theme of the poem? How is the theme the same as that of "Dulce et Decorum Est"? In what sense is it different? What are some of the factors that make the total meaning different? Consider in the two poems (a) the length and kind of sentence and (b) the choice of words. (Which poem is breezier? Why?)

8 ★ Write a short paper arguing that "Dulce et Decorum Est" is effective by what it puts in and "plato told him" by what it leaves out.

# II

# *THE POEM*

## *AS A*

# *DRAMATIC SITUATION*

**Every poem has a speaker**

i

The most important single factor in a poem considered as a dramatic situation is its speaker. A poem is always spoken by someone—most obviously, by the poet. But when we start looking closely at the dramatic character of poetry, we find that we have to allow for a more immediate speaker than the poet himself, one whom the poet has imagined speaking the poem, as an actor speaks a part written for him by a playwright. In some instances, this imagined speaker is in no way definite or distinctive; he is simply a voice. The speakers of the humorous poems that began this book, with the possible exception of the "Dog" in poem 5, are just this. But often the speaker is much more than a voice, and then he becomes a contributor to the whole meaning of the poem.

The speaker of "A Man Who Had Fallen Among Thieves" is, for example, somewhat more than a voice. He is obviously not a sentimental fellow given to splashing about in his emotions. He describes the sight before him with clinical attention to vulgar details, and even with a certain superior humor. His humor is directed partly at the victim with his "fifteenthrate" notions of an "emancipated" evening and partly at the "citizens" who (he takes pleasure in reminding us, by the words "graze" and "pastures") are as much sheep as the victim, because their ideas about what is "done" and "not done" are as fifteenthrate as the victim's idea of emancipation. All in all, we will probably feel that the speaker of the poem is like a hard-boiled newspaperman. He has seen a good deal of the seamy side of things and people, and he is perhaps not above enjoying the shocked look on the faces of the respectable when words like "trouser-fly" and "puke" are poked under their noses. Yet this is the man to whom the experience described in the poem's last stanza happens, and that it does happen to *him* is part of the poem's point. For he is tough-minded enough (as the "citizens" are not) to be able to respond to the life-giving, exalting, almost miraculous experience that arrives when he staggers, with the drunken man in his arms, toward an unknown dimension reaching beyond the stars.

The following poem also has a speaker with a definite personality.

[1]                     *The Man He Killed*
                     THOMAS HARDY (1840–1928)

              Had he and I but met
              By some old ancient inn,
          We should have sat us down to wet
              Right many a nipperkin!°

              But ranged° as infantry,                          5
              And staring face to face,
          I shot at him as he at me,
              And killed him in his place.

              I shot him dead because—
              Because he was my foe,                            10
          Just so: my foe of course he was;
              That's clear enough; although

              He thought he'd 'list,° perhaps
              Offhand-like—just as I—

---

°**nipperkin:** glass holding half a pint.      °**ranged:** set in place.      °**'list:** enlist.

Was out of work—had sold his traps—°                    15
No other reason why.

Yes; quaint and curious war is!
You shoot a fellow down
You'd treat if met where any bar is,
Or help to half-a-crown.°                    20

## QUESTIONS

1 ★ Why had the speaker enlisted?

2 ★ Would you say that in peacetime the speaker was an officeworker or a manual worker? How do you know? What shows him to be a friendly, companionable sort?

3 ★ What kind of language does he use—colloquial or formal? List three or four phrases that seem to be characteristic of his language usage. What two words in line 2 show that he is not a very precise user of language?

4 ★ What question is he trying to answer in stanza three? What answer does he give? Is it an adequate answer? What in stanzas three and four show that the speaker is not fully satisfied with it?

5 ★ What does his answer have in common with the answer of the man in "Mending Wall" (p. 8) who repeats, "Good fences make good neighbors"? Why would you not expect an answer of this kind from the speaker of "A Man Who Had Fallen Among Thieves"?

6 ★ What words in line 17 suggest there are limitations in the speaker's ability to think and feel deeply about what he has done? How does his way of dismissing the problem throw light on why decent and sensible men keep on going to war?

7 ★ Write a short paper contrasting and showing resemblances among the men who speak in "Dulce et Decorum Est," "A Man Who Had Fallen Among Thieves," and "The Man He Killed." Include evidence from the poems to support your opinions in each case.

---

°traps: belongings (the "tools of his trade").    °half-a-crown: a former British coin worth (when the poem was written) about sixty-five cents.

The following poem has a speaker whose personality is by no means as simple as that of the speaker in "The Man He Killed," but there is no doubt about the strongly personal point of view.

[2]                    *There Died a Myriad*
                   (Part V of "Hugh Selwyn Mauberley")

                   EZRA POUND (1885–      )

There died a myriad,°
And of the best, among them,
For an old bitch gone in the teeth,°
For a botched° civilization.

Charm, smiling at the good mouth,°                          5
Quick eyes gone under earth's lid,

For two gross of broken statues,
For a few thousand battered books.


## QUESTIONS

1 ★ What words show the speaker's attitude toward the dead men here? How far does this attitude resemble or differ from the attitude taken by the speaker of the preceding poem toward the man he killed? What kind of person is the speaker?

2 ★ In lines 7–8, the speaker implies that the civilization he is speaking of has little *genuine* respect for art or learning. What words in these lines especially carry this implication?

3 ★ What interests does the speaker of this poem show that would not

---

°**myriad:** a vast number.
°**For an old bitch gone in the teeth:** the connotations of "bitch," old age, and decayed teeth are all suggestive of corruption and degeneration.
°**botched:** messed up, bungled.
°**Charm, smiling at the good mouth:** The dead soldiers were young and pleasant, and smiled at pretty girls.

be apt to concern the speaker in the preceding poem? Does he use any words that the other speaker would be unlikely to use? Which?

4 ★ Would the poem be strengthened or weakened by the omission of line 3? Why? (Consider whether line 4 says the same thing or not.)

5 ★ What would be lost by omitting the word "good" in line 5? (Consider line 3.)


## ii

The following two poems have alternate speakers—a type of "dramatic situation" that very often occurs in poems.


[3]                    *Proud Maisie*
              SIR WALTER SCOTT (1771–1832)

Proud Maisie is in the wood,
Walking so early;
Sweet Robin sits on the bush
Singing so rarely.°

"Tell me, thou bonny° bird,                              5
When shall I marry me?"
"When six braw° gentlemen
Kirkward° shall carry ye."

"Who makes the bridal bed,
Birdie, say truly?"                                      10
"The gray-headed sexton
That delves the grave duly.

The glow-worm o'er grave and stone
Shall light thee steady.
The owl from the steeple sing,                           15
'Welcome, proud lady.' "

---

°**rarely:** excellently, with rare skill.    °**bonny:** pretty.    °**braw:** well-dressed.    °**Kirkward:** toward the church.

The speakers in this poem are Proud Maisie and the robin. Proud Maisie is a young girl with love on her mind, as her two questions to the robin show. She is proud with the pardonable pride that comes to all of us in extreme youth, when we seem to carry the future in our pocket like an uncashed blank check. Confident in her beauty, her thoughts turn as inevitably to marriage as the compass needle to the north. There is no shadow of doubt in her mind that the world is all hers. She does not ask *whether;* she ask *when* and *with whom.*

The other speaker, Sweet Robin, cannot in fact speak at all, and so makes the best possible speaker for this particular situation. For since his "speech" is not literal, we know that his message is one that Maisie does not hear. Maisie's ignorance, of course, is the source of the pity that we feel for her. What comes to Maisie's own ears is simply the robin singing "rarely" in the springtime. What *we* hear, on the other hand, in the robin's song, is a sentence of death. Thus the poem is a dialogue in which neither party actually says anything. Maisie does not "literally" address the robin. The nature of her questions is implicit in her bearing, her youth, her walking in the woods in the spring dawn. Nor does the robin literally reply. His answers are implicit in the world he represents— the world of nature, of which Maisie also is part, and in which the date of execution is unpredictable but the sentence is always death.

By using alternative "speakers," Scott manages to concentrate in a few lines all the feelings of pity and wonder and resignation (since there is nothing that can be done) that we feel when a young man or young woman dies. We are all part of the one nature, his poem seems to say, and the same laws that bear us toward the bridal bed (line 9) bear us also —and perhaps at any instant—to the grave (line 12).

## QUESTIONS

1 ⋆ Compare this poem with "Bredon Hill," which appears on page 11. What lines here correspond in unspoiled joyousness to lines 1–10 of "Bredon Hill"?

2 ⋆ In "Bredon Hill" our first hint that something may go counter to expectation occurs in line 11. Where does a similar hint first occur in "Proud Maisie"?

3 ⋆ In "Bredon Hill" the change in the meaning of the bells in lines 26 and 31–35 is acted out for us by changes in the description of their music and in the hearer's attitude to it. What is changed in the last two lines of "Proud Maisie" as compared with what we read in lines 3–4?

[4]                            *Piazza Piece*

JOHN CROWE RANSOM (1888–     )

—I am a gentleman in a dustcoat trying
To make you hear. Your ears are soft and small
And listen to an old man not at all,
They want the young men's whispering and sighing.
But see the roses on your trellis dying                    5
And hear the spectral° singing of the moon;
For I must have my lovely lady soon,
I am a gentleman in a dustcoat trying.

—I am a lady young in beauty waiting
Until my truelove comes, and then we kiss.                  10
But what gray man among the vines is this
Whose words are dry and faint as in a dream?
Back from my trellis, Sir, before I scream!
I am a lady young in beauty waiting.

## QUESTIONS

1 ★ Who are the two speakers here?

2 ★ In what respects does their dialogue resemble that in "Proud Maisie"?
In what respects does it differ? (Consider lines 11–14.)

3 ★ How has the meaning of "trying" in line 1 grown by the time of its
reappearance in line 8? How does the meaning of "waiting" in line 9
enlarge by the time of its reappearance in line 14? What happens to
the meaning of "dustcoat" by the time we discover who the "gentle-
man" is?

### iii

As the title indicates in the following poem, a single person is speak-
ing inside a monastery. The speaker is a monk, who is revealing his
intense hatred of another monk (the Brother Lawrence of line 3) as he
watches him working in his garden.

---

°**spectral:** ghostly.

[5]              *Soliloquy of the Spanish Cloister*
                 ROBERT BROWNING (1812–1889)

Gr-r-r—there go, my heart's abhorrence!
   Water your damned flowerpots, do!
If hate killed men, Brother Lawrence,
   God's blood, would not mine kill you!
What? your myrtle-bush wants trimming?                        5
   Oh, that rose has prior claims—
Needs its leaden vase filled brimming?
   Hell dry you up with its flames!

At the meal we sit together:
   *Salve tibi!*° I must hear                      10
Wise talk of the kind of weather,
   Sort of season, time of year:
*Not a plenteous cork-crop: scarcely*
   *Dare we hope oak-galls, I doubt:*
*What's the Latin name for "parsley"?*                        15
   What's the Greek name for Swine's Snout?

Whew! We'll have our platter burnished,
   Laid with care on our own shelf!
With a fire-new spoon we're furnished,
   And a goblet for ourself,                          20
Rinsed like something sacrificial
   Ere 'tis fit to touch our chaps—°
Marked with *L* for our initial!
   (He-he! There his lily snaps!)

*Saint,* forsooth! While brown Dolores                        25
   Squats outside the Convent bank
With Sanchicha, telling stories,
   Steeping tresses in the tank,°
Blue-black lustrous, thick like horse-hairs,
   —Can't I see his dead eye glow,                    30

---

°*Salve tibi!* Hail to you!    °**chaps:** jaws.    °**tank:** pool.

Bright as 'twere a Barbary corsair's?
    (That is, if he'd let it show!)

When he finishes refection,°
    Knife and fork he never lays
Cross-wise, to my recollection,            35
    As do I, in Jesu's praise.
I the Trinity° illustrate,
    Drinking watered orange-pulp
In three sips the Arian° frustrate;
    While he drains his at one gulp.       40

Oh, those melons! If he's able
    We're to have a feast! so nice!
One goes to the Abbot's table,
    All of us get each a slice.
How go on your flowers? None double?     45
    Not one fruit-sort can you spy?
Strange!—And I, too, at such trouble
    Keep them close-nipped on the sly!

There's a great text in Galatians,°
    Once you trip on it, entails        50
Twenty-nine distinct damnations,
    One sure, if another fails:
If I trip him just a-dying,
    Sure of heaven as sure can be,
Spin him round and send him flying     55
    Off to hell, a Manichee!°

---

°refection: meal.
°Trinity: unity of God in three persons: Father, Son, and Holy Spirit.
°Arian: follower of Arius (died A.D. 336), who denied the Trinity.
°text in Galatians: In stanza seven the speaker suggests trapping Brother Lawrence into making heretical statements, thereby damning his soul. St. Paul's letter to the Galatians is a stinging rebuke to those who would substitute rigid adherence to ritual for the true spirit of Jesus's gospel.
°Manichee: The heresy of the Manichee probably referred to here is the belief that evil is not part of God's creation. A Persian, Manes (A.D. 216?–276?), founded a religion usually called *Manichaeism*.

Or, my scrofulous° French novel
    On gray paper with blunt type!
Simply glance at it, you grovel
    Hand and foot in Belial's° gripe:°        60
If I double down its pages
    At the woeful sixteenth print,
When he gathers his greengages,°
    Ope a sieve° and slip it in't?

Or, there's Satan! one might venture       65
    Pledge one's soul to him, yet leave
Such a flaw in the indenture
    As he'd miss till, past retrieve,
Blasted lay that rose-acacia
    We're so proud of! *Hy, Zy, Hine* . . .°    70
'St, there's Vespers! *Plena gratiâ,*
    *Ave, Virgo!*° Gr-r-r—you swine!

## QUESTIONS

1 ★ In what tone of voice would the speaker say lines 5–7? What different tone would he use for lines 1–4 and line 8?

2 ★ Which of the two tones prevails in stanza three? The platter, shelf, spoons, goblet, and chaps that the speaker mentions are obviously not things he shares with Brother Lawrence; so what does his use of "we" and "our" indicate about his tone of voice here? And also in line 70?

3 ★ What kind of behavior is he ascribing to Brother Lawrence in stanza four? How do we know that it is really the speaker who indulges in such thoughts, rather than Brother Lawrence?

4 ★ Is the speaker's behavior in stanza five particularly praiseworthy, as he obviously thinks it is? What is shown about the speaker by the fact that he finds fault with Brother Lawrence's actions in this regard?

---

°**scrofulous:** diseased; here, pornographic.   °**Belial:** one of Satan's henchmen.   °**gripe:** grip.   °**greengages:** plums.   °**sieve:** meshed basket in which Brother Lawrence will put the greengages.   °***Hy, Zy, Hine:*** probably some sort of Satanic incantation.   °***Plena . . . Virgo:*** Hail, Virgin, full of grace (formal prayer).

5 ★ Stanza six tells us that the speaker has borne a grudge against Brother Lawrence for a long time. What action does the speaker refer to in lines 45–48?

6 ★ In stanzas seven, eight, and nine the speaker thinks of three schemes for revenge. One is to trick Lawrence into heresy, and the second into ill desires; the third is to bargain with Satan to destroy Brother Lawrence's favorite shrub. What is revealed about the speaker in these stanzas? For instance, why is it significant that in line 54 he admits that Brother Lawrence is as "sure of heaven as sure can be," and that in line 62 the speaker reveals that he knows exactly where the "woeful" print (illustration) *is*, in *his* "French novel"? What, in particular, does his third scheme indicate about the extent of his jealousy and hatred?

7 ★ Just what is it in Brother Lawrence that the speaker detests? Has the speaker revealed anything about the man that is detestable? How do we know that Brother Lawrence is probably as "sure of heaven as sure can be"? What has the speaker revealed about himself?

## The speaker of a poem speaks from a personal situation

### i

The personal situation in any poem is whatever the speaker of the poem is reacting to. We can easily illustrate this fact from the poems we have read in the preceding sections. In "Mending Wall" (p. 8) the situation is the springtime walking of the boundary line by two farmers. In "A Man Who Had Fallen Among Thieves" (p. 15), the situation is the disheveled, drunken fellow in the dirt, looked at and then abandoned by the "staunch" and "leal" passersby who live at respectable addresses. In "Proud Maisie" (p. 34) the situation for Maisie is the happy spring morning with its natural suggestions of marriage, and the situation for Sweet Robin is the sight of a young girl, beautiful and doomed. What is the situation for each of the speakers in "Piazza Piece" (p. 36)?

What is the situation for each of the speakers in the following poem?

[ 1 ]                    *A Kind of Good-bye*

THEODORE SPENCER (1902–1949)

I met an old man near a darkened house,
And he looked in my eyes and spoke of that house,

Said the girl with flame in her voice, in her hair.
"What did he say to you standing there?
What did he say to you, darling, darling?"                          5

He said that the house was my own house;
Said the girl with flame in her eyes, in her hair;
That's what he said to me standing there;
That's what he said to me, darling, darling.

He said I'd live all day in that house,                             10
He said I'd live all night in that house,
Said the girl with flame in her hands, in her hair;
"And what did you answer him standing there?
What did you answer him, darling, darling?"

I said I hated my darkened house,                                   15
Said the girl with the flame in her skin, in her hair.
That's what I said to him standing there;
That's what I said to him, darling, darling.

But the old man told me to enter that house;
"You are here; we are ready; come into your house";                 20
He told me to enter my darkened house,
Said the girl with flame in her heart, in her hair.
That's what he said to me standing there;
That's what he said to me, darling, darling.

## QUESTIONS

1 ★ What is the darkened house? Who is the old man? In "Piazza Piece"
the "gray man" (line 11) is contrasted with "my truelove" (line 10).
Who is contrasted in the same way with the "old man" in "A Kind of
Good-bye"?

2 ★ How, in a sense, does the "flame" gradually devour the girl as the
stanzas progress?

3 ★ What resemblance has this poem to "Bredon Hill," which you read
on page 11?

What is the situation to which the speaker is reacting in the following poem?

[ 2 ]                    *Porphyria's Lover*

ROBERT BROWNING (1812–1889)

The rain set early in tonight,
    The sullen wind was soon awake,
It tore the elm-tops down for spite,
    And did its best to vex the lake;
I listened with heart fit to break;       5
When glided in Porphyria; straight
    She shut the cold out and the storm,
And kneeled and made the cheerless grate
    Blaze up, and all the cottage warm;
Which done, she rose and from her form    10
Withdrew the dripping cloak and shawl,
    And laid her soiled gloves by, untied
Her hat, and let the damp hair fall,
    And, last, she sat down by my side
And called me. When no voice replied,    15
She put my arm about her waist,
    And made her smooth white shoulder bare,
And all her yellow hair displaced,
    And, stooping, made my cheek lie there,
And spread, o'er all, her yellow hair,    20
Murmuring how she loved me—she
    Too weak, for all her heart's endeavor,
To set its struggling passion free
    From pride, and vainer ties dissever,
And give herself to me for ever.    25
But passion sometimes would prevail,
    Nor could tonight's gay feast restrain
A sudden thought of one so pale
    For love of her, and all in vain:

So, she was come through wind and rain. 30
Be sure I looked up at her eyes
    Happy and proud; at last I knew
Porphyria worshipped me; surprise
    Made my heart swell, and still it grew
While I debated what to do. 35
That moment she was mine, mine, fair,
    Perfectly pure and good: I found
A thing to do, and all her hair
    In one long yellow string I wound
Three times her little throat around, 40
And strangled her. No pain felt she;
    I am quite sure she felt no pain.
As a shut bud that holds a bee,
    I warily oped her lids: again
Laughed the blue eyes without a strain. 45
And I untightened next the tress
    About her neck; her cheek once more
Blushed bright beneath my burning kiss:
    I propped her head up as before,
Only, this time my shoulder bore 50
Her head, which droops upon it still:
    The smiling rosy little head,
So glad it has its utmost will,
    That all it scorned at once is fled,
And I, its love, am gained instead! 55
Porphyria's love: she guessed not how
    Her darling one wish would be heard.
And thus we sit together now,
    And all night long we have not stirred,
And yet God has not said a word! 60

## QUESTIONS

1 * What is the personal situation of Porphyria in this poem? Why does
her lover think her "weak" (line 22)? To what sorts of things does he

probably refer in "vainer ties" (line 24)? What do you think of her
from the actions ascribed to her in the poem?

2 ★ What is the personal situation of the speaker? Why does he do what
he does? Step by step, trace the way in which his state of mind is
made known to us. What is the effect of lines 58–60?


## ii
What is the situation of the speakers in the following three poems? What
are they reacting to?


[3]                          *Ulysses*
              ALFRED, LORD TENNYSON (1809–1892)

It little profits that an idle king,°
By this still hearth, among these barren crags,
Matched with an agèd wife, I mete and dole
Unequal laws unto a savage race,
That hoard, and sleep, and feed, and know not me.          5
I cannot rest from travel. I will drink
Life to the lees. All times I have enjoyed
Greatly, have suffered greatly, both with those
That loved me, and alone; on shore, and when
Through scudding drifts the rainy Hyades°                   10
Vext the dim sea. I am become a name;
For always roaming with a hungry heart
Much have I seen and known,—cities of men
And manners, climates, councils, governments,
Myself not least, but honored of them all,—                15
And drunk delight of battle with my peers,
Far on the ringing plains of windy Troy.
I am a part of all that I have met;

---

°**idle king:** Ulysses, after the Trojan War and his years of adventure before
   reaching his home island, Ithaca.
°**Hyades:** star group, supposedly bringer of rain.

Yet all experience is an arch where-through
Gleams that untraveled world, whose margin fades          20
Forever and forever when I move.
How dull it is to pause, to make an end,
To rust unburnished, not to shine in use!
As though to breathe were life! Life piled on life
Were all too little, and of one to me                     25
Little remains; but every hour is saved
From that eternal silence, something more,
A bringer of new things; and vile it were
For some three suns to store and hoard myself,
And this gray spirit yearning in desire                   30
To follow knowledge like a sinking star,
Beyond the utmost bound of human thought.

This is my son, mine own Telemachus,
To whom I leave the scepter and the isle—
Well-loved of me, discerning to fulfill                   35
This labor, by slow prudence to make mild
A rugged people, and through soft degrees
Subdue them to the useful and the good.
Most blameless is he, centered in the sphere
Of common duties, decent not to fail                      40
In offices of tenderness, and pay
Meet adoration to my household gods,
When I am gone. He works his work, I mine.

There lies the port; the vessel puffs her sail;
There gloom the dark, broad seas. My mariners,           45
Souls that have toiled, and wrought, and thought with me,—
That ever with a frolic welcome took
The thunder and the sunshine, and opposed
Free hearts, free foreheads,—you and I are old;
Old age hath yet his honor and his toil.                  50
Death closes all; but something ere the end,
Some work of noble note, may yet be done,

Not unbecoming men that strove with gods.
The lights begin to twinkle from the rocks;
The long day wanes: the slow moon climbs; the deep°          55
Moans round with many voices. Come, my friends.
'Tis not too late to seek a newer world.
Push off, and sitting well in order° smite
The sounding furrows; for my purpose holds
To sail beyond the sunset, and the baths°          60
Of all the western stars, until I die.
It may be that the gulfs will wash us down;
It may be we shall touch the Happy Isles,°
And see the great Achilles,° whom we knew.
Though much is taken, much abides; and though          65
We are not now that strength which in old days
Moved earth and heaven, that which we are, we are,—
One equal temper of heroic hearts,
Made weak by time and fate, but strong in will
To strive, to seek, to find, and not to yield.          70

## QUESTIONS

1 ★ What is the situation of the speaker? Why is he an "idle king" now? What is it he does not like about his situation? What has his past been like? What do lines 3–5, 11, 13–15, 22–23, and 39–43 in particular tell us about the kind of man he is?

2 ★ To whom is he speaking? What do the speaker and his audience have in common? What are they doing while he is speaking to them? Why is it suitable that they should set off in the waning of the day?

3 ★ Try to state specifically what attitudes of heart and mind Ulysses is meant to stand for, in the poem.

---

°deep: sea.    °sitting . . . order: Ulysses's ship is a galley; the oarsmen sit in rows.    °baths: i.e., the seas into which the stars seem to sink. °Happy Isles: Greek heroes' heaven.    °Achilles: greatest of the Greek warriors at Troy.

[4] *Edward*

ANONYMOUS

"Why dois° your brand° sae drap wi bluid,°
    Edward, Edward,
Why dois your brand sae drap wi bluid,
    And why sae sad gang° yee O?"
"O I hae killed my hauke sae guid,°                    5
    Mither, mither,
O I hae killed my hauke sae guid,
    And I had nae mair° bot° hee O."

"Your haukis bluid was nevir sae reid,°
    Edward, Edward,                                    10
Your haukis bluid was nevir sae reid,
    My deir son I tell thee O."
"O I hae killed my reid-roan steid,
    Mither, mither,
O I hae killed my reid-roan steid,                     15
    That erst° was sae fair and frie° O."

"Your steid was auld, and ye hae got mair,
    Edward, Edward,
Your steid was auld, and ye hae got mair,
    Sum other dule ye drie° O."                        20
"O I hae killed my fadir deir,
    Mither, mither,
O I hae killed my fadir deir,
    Alas, and wae° is mee O!"

"And whatten penance wul° ye drie for that,           25
    Edward, Edward,

---

°**dois:** does.    °**brand:** sword.    °**bluid:** blood.    °**gang:** go.    °**guid:** good.
°**mair:** more.    °**bot:** but.    °**reid:** red.    °**erst:** once.    °**frie:** spirited.
°**dule ye drie:** grief you suffer.    °**wae:** woe.    °**wul:** will.

And whatten penance wul ye drie for that?
　　My deir son, now tell me O."
"Ile set my feit in yonder boat,
　　　　Mither, mither,
Ile set my feit in yonder boat,                    30
　　And Ile fare ovir the sea O."

"And what wul ye doe wi your towirs and your ha,°
　　　　Edward, Edward?
And what wul ye doe wi your towirs and your ha,    35
　　That were sae fair to see O?"
"Ile let thame stand tul they doun fa,
　　　　Mither, mither,
Ile let thame stand tul they doun fa,
　　For here nevir mair maun° I bee O."           40

"And what wul ye leive to your bairns° and your wife,
　　　　Edward, Edward?
And what wul ye leive to your bairns and your wife,
　　Whan ye gang ovir the sea O?"
"The warldis° room, late them beg thrae° life,    45
　　　　Mither, mither,
The warldis room, late them beg thrae life,
　　For thame nevir mair wul I see O."

"And what wul ye leive to your ain° mither deir,·
　　　　Edward, Edward?                          50
And what wul ye leive to your ain mither deir?
　　My deir son, now tell me O."
"The curse of hell frae me sall° ye beir,°
　　　　Mither, mither,
The curse of hell frae me sall ye beir,           55
　　Sic° counseils ye gave to me O."

---

°**ha:** hall.　　°**maun:** must.　　°**bairns:** children.　　°**warldis:** world's.
°**thrae:** through.　　°**ain:** own.　　°**sall:** shall.　　°**beir:** bear.　　°**sic:** such.

QUESTIONS

1 ★ From what situation does Edward speak? How recently has he done the deed? What details are added to our realization of the situation, and to his, by the questions in stanzas four, five, and six? How does the gradual realization help account for the outburst in stanza seven?

2 ★ From what situation does the mother seemingly speak in the beginning? What clues gradually lead us to wonder if this is the whole truth? When do we discover her true situation? When does she discover it? How do we know it was not what she expected?

3 ★ Discuss some of the advantages of using two speakers in this poem.

[5]     *La Belle Dame sans Merci°*
        JOHN KEATS (1795–1821)

Ah, what can ail thee, wretched wight,°
    Alone and palely loitering;°
The sedge° is withered from the lake,
    And no birds sing.

Ah, what can ail thee, wretched wight,                    5
    So haggard and so woebegone?
The squirrel's granary is full,
    And the harvest's done.

I see a lily on thy brow,
    With anguish moist and fever dew;                     10
And on thy cheek a fading rose
    Fast withereth too.

I met a lady in the meads
    Full beautiful, a faery's child;
Her hair was long, her foot was light,                    15
    And her eyes were wild.

---

°Title: the beautiful lady without mercy.    °wight: creature.    °loitering: moving about aimlessly.    °sedge: marsh grass.

I set her on my pacing steed,
    And nothing else saw all day long;
For sideways would she lean, and sing
    A faery's song.                                                    20

I made a garland for her head,
    And bracelets too, and fragrant zone;°
She looked at me as she did love,
    And made sweet moan.

She found me roots of relish sweet,                                    25
    And honey wild, and manna dew;°
And sure in language strange she said,
    I love thee true.

She took me to her elfin grot,°
    And there she gazed and sighèd deep,                               30
And there I shut her wild sad eyes—
    So kissed to sleep.

And there we slumbered on the moss,
    And there I dreamed, ah woe betide,°
The latest° dream I ever dreamed                                       35
    On the cold hill side.

I saw pale kings, and princes too,
    Pale warriors, death-pale were they all;
Who cried—"La belle Dame sans merci
    Hath thee in thrall!" °                                            40

---

°**zone:** sash.
°**honey ... dew:** John the Baptist lived on wild honey in the wilderness; manna is the food that the Israelites received miraculously in their time of trial in the wilderness; together with "roots of relish sweet," the food here ironically seems somehow of an unearthly kind that leaves the "wretched wight" unable to take any normal nourishment (all of which is consistent with the lady's bewitchment).
°**grot:** cave.     °**betide:** befall.     °**latest:** last.     °**thrall:** servitude.

I saw their starved lips in the gloam
   With horrid warning gapèd wide,
And I awoke, and found me here
   On the cold hill side.

And this is why I sojourn here        45
   Alone and palely loitering,
Though the sedge is withered from the lake,
   And no birds sing.

## QUESTIONS

1 ⋆ Who are the two speakers in the poem? When does the second speaker begin?

2 ⋆ What is the personal situation out of which the "wretched wight" speaks? What did he hope for from the lady he had met "in the meads"? What did he receive from her? What do the paleness stressed in lines 2, 11, and 37–38 and the "starved lips" of line 41 tell us about the nature of the lady and what she does to her victims? By what wiles did she get the principal speaker "in thrall"? In what sense has he consciously chosen his own doom?

3 ⋆ How is his personal situation (his spiritual situation, perhaps) underscored by the physical situation in which he is found "loitering"? How is the autumn appropriate to this story, as sunset is to the story of "Ulysses"? Consider what the shortened fourth line of each stanza (basically the ballad form) contributes to the sense of barrenness and lifelessness.

## The speaker of a poem speaks to some kind of audience

i

We have used previous poems to illustrate the fact that every poem has a speaker, and we can also use previous poems to illustrate the fact that this speaker is addressing an audience. The only problem is that of deciding whether the audience is a person or persons imagined in the poem (for instance, the person called "darling" in "A Kind of Good-bye") or a group of hearers or readers altogether outside it—in short, us. In the same way, as we saw earlier, the speaker may vary from a person imagined in the poem to a "voice" altogether outside it—in short, the poet. In a literal sense, of course, the poet himself always stands behind any imagined speaker and speaks through him, just as we always stand beyond any imagined audience and listen through it.

In the following poem by Robert Herrick (as in "Proud Maisie," "Piazza Piece," "A Kind of Good-bye," "Edward," "La Belle Dame sans Merci," and all other poems with two speakers), there are actually *three* audiences: the rose, the young lady to whom the rose is being sent, and we—the hearers or readers.

[1]                              *To the Rose*

ROBERT HERRICK (1591–1674)

Go, happy rose, and interwove
With other flowers, bind my love.
   Tell her, too, she must not be
   Longer flowing, longer free,
   That so oft has fettered° me.                              5

Say, if she's fretful, I have bands
Of pearl and gold, to bind her hands;
   Tell her, if she struggle still,
   I have myrtle° rods, at will,
   For to tame, though not to kill.                          10

Take thou my blessing thus, and go,
And tell her this—but do not so,
   Lest a handsome anger fly
   Like a lightning from her eye,
   And burn thee up, as well as I.                           15

QUESTIONS

1 ★ What are the "bands of pearl and gold" in lines 6–7? What are the "rods" in line 9? How fearsome a rod would myrtle make?

---

°**fettered:** bound, tied up.   °**myrtle:** a flowering vine sacred to Venus, goddess of love.

2 ⋆ What does the speaker gain by pretending to address the rose and letting the lady overhear? Why will she be pleased that he calls the rose "happy" (line 1)? What is the resemblance between this poem and Pope's "Epigram" (p. 5)?

3 ⋆ Why does the speaker change his mind in line 12? Or does he?

4 ⋆ Behind this poem lies the custom of sending an ambassador with instructions. How does this custom heighten the compliment involved?

## ii

Consider the question of audience(s) in the three following poems.

[2]                          *Song, To Celia*
                    BEN JONSON (1572–1637)

Drink to me only with thine eyes,
      And I will pledge with mine;
Or leave a kiss but in the cup,
      And I'll not look for wine.
The thirst that from the soul doth rise                    5
      Doth ask a drink divine;
But might I of Jove's nectar sup,
      I would not change for thine.

I sent thee late a rosy wreath,
      Not so much honoring thee,                            10
As giving it a hope that there
      It could not withered be.
But thou thereon didst only breathe,
      And sent'st it back to me,
Since when it grows and smells, I swear,                   15
      Not of itself, but thee.

## QUESTIONS

1 ⋆ This poem is a series of compliments addressed to an audience of one. The basis of these compliments in the first stanza is the action of drink-

ing healths. Who are the drinkers in this instance? What in fact are they drinking besides wine? What compliment is paid to the lady in lines 1–4? In lines 5–8? In what sense can the first stanza be considered an expanding compliment?

2 ★ What is the basis of the compliment in the second stanza? In what sense is the second stanza even more complimentary to the lady than the first one is?

3 ★ What response do you suppose the speaker hopes for from his audience of one?

[ 3 ]                    *Holy Sonnet 14*

JOHN DONNE (1572–1631)

Batter my heart, three-personed God; for you
As yet but knock, breathe, shine, and seek to mend.
That I may rise and stand, o'erthrow me and bend
Your force to break, blow, burn, and make me new.
I, like an usurped town, to another due,                          5
Labor to admit you, but, oh, to no end;
Reason, your viceroy in me, me should defend,
But is captived and proves weak or untrue.

Yet dearly I love you and would be lovèd fain,
But am betrothed unto your enemy:                                10
Divorce me, untie or break that knot again,
Take me to you, imprison me, for I,
Except you enthrall me, never shall be free,
Nor ever chaste, except you ravish me.

QUESTIONS

1 ★ To what does the speaker compare himself and to what does he compare God in lines 1–4? in lines 5–8? in lines 9–14? How are these metaphors related? In other words, what manner of action is common to all of them? Would it make any difference if they were introduced in any other order? Explain.

2 * The prayer is filled with what seem to be contradictions—e.g. "That I may rise and stand, o'erthrow me" (line 3). Find at least two more such contradictions in lines 12–14. Is there a similar contradiction in the very idea of asking God to use force on us? Why will God's force be necessary? (Consider who the *usurper* is in line 5 and who the *enemy* is in line 10.)

3 * A well-known Christian prayer, speaking of God, ends: "Whose service is perfect freedom." How can *service* be *freedom?* How does this contradiction relate to those in Donne's poem?

4 * Write a paragraph arguing that the speaker really addresses his poem to two audiences: (a) God (b) himself.


[ 4 ]                          *To a Mouse*
On Turning Her Up in Her Nest with the Plough, November, 1785

ROBERT BURNS (1759–1796)

Wee, sleekit,° cowrin, tim'rous beastie,
O, what a panic's in thy breastie!
Thou need na start awa sae° hasty,
    Wi' bickering° brattle!°
I wad be laith° to rin an' chase thee,      5
    Wi' murd'ring pattle!°

I'm truly sorry Man's dominion
Has broken Nature's social union,
An' justifies that ill opinion
    Which makes thee startle      10
At me, thy poor, earth-born companion,
    An' fellow-mortal!

I doubt na, whyles,° but thou may thieve.
What then? poor beastie, thou maun° live!

---

°**sleekit:** sleek. °**sae:** so. °**bickering:** scurrying. °**brattle:** clatter.
°**laith:** loath. °**pattle:** an instrument for pushing chunks of dirt, etc., off the plow. °**whyles:** on occasion. °**maun:** must.

A daimen° icker° in a thrave°                              15
    'S a sma' request.
I'll get a blessin wi' the lave,°
    And never miss't!

Thy wee bit housie, too, in ruin!
Its silly wa's° the win's are strewin!                     20
An' naething, now, to big° a new ane,
    O' foggage° green!
An' bleak December's winds ensuin,
    Baith snell ° and keen!

Thou saw the fields laid bare an' waste,                   25
An' weary Winter comin fast,
An' cozie here, beneath the blast,
    Thou thought to dwell,
Till crash! the cruel coulter° past
    Out thro' thy cell.                                30

That wee bit heap o' leaves an' stibble,°
Has cost thee mony a weary nibble!
Now thou's turned out, for a' thy trouble,
    But° house or hald,°
To thole° the Winter's sleety dribble,                     35
    An' cranreuch° cauld!

But, Mousie, thou are no thy lane,°
In proving foresight may be vain:
The best-laid schemes o' Mice an' Men,
    Gang aft a-gley,°                                  40
An' lea'e us nought but grief and pain,
    For promised joy.

---

°daimen: occasional.    °icker: ear of corn.    °thrave: twenty-four sheaves.
°lave: rest.    °wa's: walls.    °big: build.    °foggage: moss.    °snell:
piercing.    °coulter: the cutter on the plow.    °stibble: stubble.    °But:
without.    °hald: hold, protecting shelter.    °thole: bear.    °cranreuch:
hoarfrost.    °no thy lane: not alone.    °Gang aft a-gley: go oft awry.

> Still thou art blest, compared wi' me!
> The present only toucheth thee;
> But, Och! I backward cast my e'e,°                                    45
>            On prospects drear!
> An' forward, tho' I canna see,
>            I guess an' fear!

## QUESTIONS

1 ★ Who is addressing the mouse and under what circumstances? What is his attitude toward the mouse? How do you know?

2 ★ Stanzas seven and eight put the incident in a larger context than the details of the first six stanzas have suggested. What is the shift in audience, despite the fact that the speaker is still addressing the mouse? What relevance have the first six stanzas to this shift?

3 ★ What is the advantage of pretending to say everything directly to the mouse? (Retell the incident in your own words as if you were the speaker telling it, not to the mouse but to a friend.)

## Every poem is characterized by a distinctive tone

### i

The tone of a poem, like its meaning, is the consequence of all its elements sounding together like matched bells. But the most important single influence on tone is the speaker's consciousness of his situation and his audience. Let us look again at Herrick's poem on page 52. Its *speaker* is obviously a lover—any young lover; his character beyond this remains largely undefined. The speaker's *situation* is the love affair with the young lady, who, though she has long captivated the lover (line 5), has not become his captive in turn. Now he will make a strong plea—accompanied by the gift of a garland to "bind" her—that she consent to become bound in love to him. The speaker's *audiences* are, as we have noticed already, the rose in the garland, the young lady, and we. How shall we estimate the tone?

A first clue to the tone is revealed in the first two lines. The speaker sends this flowery garland in order that his love may see that bonds are not to be feared; and he calls the rose "happy" (line 1) because as part

---

°e'e: eye.

of the garland it will have the luck to embrace and bind her, as he would like to do. There is, in short, a marked youthful tenderness in the tone with which the speaker meets his situation and his audience. But along with the tenderness go other attitudes and feelings, just as other flowers accompany the rose. His suggestion about taming her with "rods" of myrtle is a bit of comic whimsy, a little joke. Rods made out of myrtle would actually be only vinelike tendrils, which would never hurt, though they might, like the garland, bind. The handcuffs made of pearl and gold are also a piece of whimsy: what the speaker means is bridal rings and bracelets. The last stanza summarizes all aspects of the poem's tone. We have its tenderness in "Take thou my blessing thus, and go"; the comic whimsy in the mock fear of being burned to death by the "lightning" of her eye; and under it all, since the fear is not *entirely* mock, the lover's zeal to win at last the love for which he longs.

Following is a passage of dialogue from Shakespeare's play *Romeo and Juliet*. It represents the moment of the lovers' first meeting, when both are struck with love at first sight, at an evening masquerade ball in Juliet's home. Romeo, dressed as a "palmer"—a pilgrim to a holy shrine—proceeds to address Juliet as if she were a saint whose shrine he has at last reached; and she, taking the cue, replies in the same way. By line 14 he has kissed her, and by line 18 he has kissed her again. The variations of tone in the lovers' speech as they progress to their first embrace (almost as in a dream) are worth close examination.

[ 1 ]              From *Romeo and Juliet,* I, v
                WILLIAM SHAKESPEARE (1564–1616)

ROMEO    If I profane with my unworthiest hand
         This holy shrine, the gentle sin is this,
         My lips, two blushing pilgrims, ready stand
         To smooth that rough touch with a tender kiss.
JULIET   Good pilgrim, you do wrong your hand too much,       5
         Which mannerly devotion shows in this;
         For saints have hands that pilgrims' hands do touch,
         And palm to palm is holy palmers' kiss.
ROMEO    Have not saints lips, and holy palmers too?
JULIET   Ay, pilgrim, lips that they must use in prayer.       10
ROMEO    O, then, dear saint, let lips do what hands do;

They pray; grant thou, lest faith turn to despair.
JULIET   Saints do not move,° though grant for prayers' sake.
ROMEO   Then move not, while my prayer's effect I take.
Thus from my lips by thine my sin is purged.                    15
JULIET   Then have my lips the sin that they have took.
ROMEO   Sin from my lips? O trespass sweetly urged!
Give me my sin again.

## QUESTIONS

1 ★ In what way does the tone of the Shakespearean passage resemble that of "To the Rose"? Are there any differences? How do you think the tone of the Shakespearean passage is affected by the presence of two speakers?

2 ★ What does the pilgrim–saint situation contribute to the tone?

3 ★ Why do the pilgrim-lips blush? Because the shrine has been profaned? Because they are the color that all lips are? Because of the proposal they are now making? Or all three? Explain.

4 ★ What differing senses does "devotion" (line 6) have here? Consider it first as a religious term and then as a lover's. What about "faith" (line 12)? "Despair" (line 12)? "Sin" (lines 2, 15, 16, 17, 18)? What does Juliet mean by "move" in line 13? What does Romeo mean by it in line 14?

In Robert Browning's "In a Gondola," at the top of the next page, there is another scene between lovers. In this scene, however, there is only one speaker.

[2]                              From *In a Gondola*
                            ROBERT BROWNING (1812–1898)

The moth's kiss first!
Kiss me as if you made believe
You were not sure, this eve,
How my face, your flower, had pursed

---

°**move:** begin, make the first move.

Its petals up; so, here and there 5
You brush it, till I grow more aware
Who wants me, and wide ope I burst.

The bee's kiss, now!
Kiss me as if you entered gay
My heart at some noonday, 10
A bud that dares not disallow
The claim, so all is rendered up.
And passively its shattered cup
Over your head to sleep I bow.

## QUESTIONS

1 ★ Who speaks in the passage from "In a Gondola"—lady or man? In what situation? (For instance, would you say they had just met?) With what tone?

2 ★ How would you distinguish the tone of this poem from that of "To the Rose"? From that of the Shakespearean passage?

Compare the following poem carefully with the passage from *Romeo and Juliet*.

[3]                                *The Nun*

JAMES HENRY LEIGH HUNT (1784–1859)

If you become a nun, dear,
A friar I will be;
In any cell you run, dear,
Pray look behind for me.
The roses all turn pale, too; 5
The doves all take the veil, too;
The blind will see the show:
What! you become a nun, my dear!
I'll not believe it, no.

If you become a nun, dear,                            10
The bishop love will be;
The cupids every one, dear,
Will chant, "We trust in thee":
The incense will go sighing,
The candles fall a-dying,                             15
The water turn to wine:
What! you go take the vows, my dear!
You may—but they'll be mine.


## QUESTIONS

1 ★ What kind of man would you say the speaker of this poem is? What evidence do you find that he is unpleasantly sure of himself? How do lines 3–4 indicate that he has a childish view of the life led by friars and nuns?

2 ★ Lines 5–7 say that a lot of other "miracles" will as soon take place as the miracle of his dear's becoming a nun. What are these other miracles? What are they in stanza two?

3 ★ Do the terms adopted from religion have the same effect on tone in this poem as in the Shakespearean passage? Which poem shows more respect for religious terms? Are there any religious references in the Shakespearean passage that make you uncomfortable? Are there in "The Nun"?


ii

Here are eight more poems on which to try your ear for tone. Consider in each case the speaker(s), the situation, the audience(s), and, in general, the language.


[4]                    *Apparently with No Surprise*
                       EMILY DICKINSON (1830–1886)

Apparently with no surprise
To any happy flower,

The frost beheads it at its play
In accidental power.

The blond assassin passes on,       5
The sun proceeds unmoved
To measure off another day
For an approving God.

[5]           *"Out, Out—"*

ROBERT FROST (1874–1963)

The buzz-saw snarled and rattled in the yard
And made dust and dropped stove-length sticks of wood,
Sweet-scented stuff when the breeze drew across it.
And from there those that lifted eyes could count
Five mountain ranges one behind the other       5
Under the sunset far into Vermont.
And the saw snarled and rattled, snarled and rattled,
As it ran light, or had to bear a load.
And nothing happened: day was all but done.
Call it a day, I wish they might have said       10
To please the boy by giving him the half hour
That a boy counts so much when saved from work.
His sister stood beside them in her apron
To tell them "Supper." At the word, the saw,
As if to prove saws knew what supper meant,       15
Leaped out at the boy's hand, or seemed to leap—
He must have given the hand. However it was,
Neither refused the meeting. But the hand!
The boy's first outcry was a rueful laugh,
As he swung toward them holding up the hand       20
Half in appeal, but half as if to keep
The life from spilling. Then the boy saw all—
Since he was old enough to know, big boy
Doing a man's work, though a child at heart—

He saw all spoiled. "Don't let him cut my hand off—                    25
The doctor, when he comes. Don't let him, sister!"
So. But the hand was gone already.
The doctor put him in the dark of ether.
He lay and puffed his lips out with his breath.
And then—the watcher at his pulse took fright.                         30
No one believed. They listened at his heart.
Little—less—nothing! and that ended it.
No more to build on there. And they, since they
Were not the one dead, turned to their affairs.


[6]                        From *Macbeth,* V, v

               WILLIAM SHAKESPEARE (1564-1616)

          She should have died hereafter;
       There would have been a time for such a word.
       Tomorrow, and tomorrow, and tomorrow,
       Creeps in this petty pace from day to day,
       To the last syllable of recorded time;                          5
       And all our yesterdays have lighted fools
       The way to dusty death. Out, out, brief candle!
       Life's but a walking shadow, a poor player
       That struts and frets his hour upon the stage
       And then is heard no more. It is a tale                         10
       Told by an idiot, full of sound and fury,
       Signifying nothing.


## QUESTIONS

1 ★ The three selections (4, 5, and 6) you have just read have a theme in
    common. What is it?

2 ★ The third selection is spoken by Shakespeare's Macbeth when his hold
    on the throne of Scotland, which (with the encouragement of his wife)
    he has murdered his king to obtain, is threatened on all sides by the

enemies his crimes have made for him. Now, in addition, the news of his wife's death is brought to him. How does this knowledge affect our understanding of the tone of the passage; in other words, in view of the situation what would you have expected the tone to be? Remorseful? Defiant? What is it actually?

3 ⋆ To what phrase in the passage from Shakespeare does the title of poem 5 refer? How does our recognition of this allusion to *Macbeth* affect our understanding of the meaning of "Out, Out—"? Does it warn us not to take "Out, Out—" as the verdict of Robert Frost on life?

4 ⋆ Which two of these selections have the most in common as to tone? Which two have the least? How do you know?

5 ⋆ In what way does the theme of "Apparently with No Surprise" resemble the theme of "Proud Maisie" (p. 34)? What *additional* problem does it raise (consider the references to "accidental power," to the sun proceeding "unmoved," and to "an approving God")? Where is the same problem raised in "Out, Out—" and the *Macbeth* passage?


[7]                    *Channel Firing*

                    THOMAS HARDY (1840–1928)

        That night your great guns, unawares,
        Shook all our coffins as we lay,
        And broke the chancel window-squares,
        We thought it was the Judgment-day

        And sat upright. While drearisome                    5
        Arose the howl of wakened hounds:
        The mouse let fall the altar-crumb,
        The worms drew back into the mounds,

        The glebe cow° drooled. Till God called, "No;
        It's gunnery practice out at sea                    10
        Just as before you went below;
        The world is as it used to be:

---

°**glebe cow:** *glebe* refers to land belonging to a parish church; the cow also belongs to the church.

"All nations striving strong to make
Red war yet redder. Mad as hatters°
They do no more for Christés° sake                          15
Than you who are helpless in such matters.

"That this is not the judgment-hour
For some of them's a blessed thing,
For if it were they'd have to scour
Hell's floor for so much threatening . . .                 20

"Ha, ha. It will be warmer when
I blow the trumpet (if indeed
I ever do; for you are men,
And rest eternal sorely need)."

So down we lay again. "I wonder,                            25
Will the world ever saner be,"
Said one, "than when He sent us under
In our indifferent century!"

And many a skeleton shook his head.
"Instead of preaching forty year,"                          30
My neighbor Parson Thirdly said,
"I wish I had stuck to pipes and beer."

Again the guns disturbed the hour,
Roaring their readiness to avenge,
As far inland as Stourton Tower,°                           35
And Camelot,° and starlit Stonehenge.°

---

°**Mad as hatters:** a common expression that means "completely zany."
°**Cristés:** Middle English spelling; along with later references to ancient
Britain, it suggests the timelessness of warlike behavior.
°**Stourton Tower:** a tower in Wiltshire, England, commemorating King
Alfred's successes against Danish invaders in the ninth century.
°**Camelot:** King Arthur's castle and court.
°**Stonehenge:** ancient ruins on Salisbury Plain in England.

QUESTIONS

1 ★ The poem was written in 1914, on the eve of the First World War. The Channel referred to is the English Channel between England and France. Who is being addressed in line 1? Who is speaking? What has disturbed the speaker? Who else responds to the noise of the "great guns," and what kind of responses are made?

2 ★ What kind of answer does God give to the speaker's question about "Judgment-day"? What is the tone of His answer? How is it consistent with the rather casual, even whimsical, behavior of the coffin-dwellers before and after He speaks? The subject matter of the poem is the ages-long eagerness of humanity to make "red war yet redder." What is significant about the fact that such a serious indictment of human behavior is made in such a lighthearted, joking way?

3 ★ In what ways does the tone shift in the last stanza? Why are Camelot, Stourton Tower, and Stonehenge referred to?

[8]                       *Mr. Flood's Party*

EDWIN ARLINGTON ROBINSON (1869–1935)

Old Eben Flood, climbing alone one night
Over the hill between the town below
And the forsaken upland hermitage
That held as much as he should ever know
On earth again of home, paused warily.                                    5
The road was his with not a native near;
And Eben, having leisure, said aloud,
For no man else in Tilbury Town to hear:

"Well, Mr. Flood, we have the harvest moon
Again, and we may not have many more;                                     10
The bird is on the wing, the poet says,
And you and I have said it here before.
Drink to the bird." He raised up to the light
The jug that he had gone so far to fill,
And answered huskily: "Well, Mr. Flood,                                   15
Since you propose it, I believe I will."

Alone, as if enduring to the end
A valiant armor of scarred hopes outworn,
He stood there in the middle of the road
Like Roland's ghost winding a silent horn.°                    20
Below him, in the town among the trees,
Where friends of other days had honored him,
A phantom salutation of the dead
Rang thinly till old Eben's eyes were dim.

Then, as a mother lays her sleeping child                       25
Down tenderly, fearing it may awake,
He set the jug down slowly at his feet
With trembling care, knowing that most things break;
And only when assured that on firm earth
It stood, as the uncertain lives of men                         30
Assuredly did not, he paced away,
And with his hand extended paused again:

"Well, Mr. Flood, we have not met like this
In a long time; and many a change has come
To both of us, I fear, since last it was                        35
We had a drop together. Welcome home!"
Convivially returning with himself,
Again he raised the jug up to the light;
And with an acquiescent quaver said:
"Well, Mr. Flood, if you insist, I might.                       40

"Only a very little, Mr. Flood—
For auld lang syne. No more, sir; that will do."
So, for the time, apparently it did,
And Eben evidently thought so too;
For soon amid the silver loneliness                             45

---

°**Like . . . horn:** Roland is the hero of the medieval French *Song of Roland:*
a man who holds the Spanish passes against the invading Moslems till one
by one his men are killed and at last he himself—but not before he has
succeeded in alerting the army of Charlemagne by successive blasts on his
great horn.

Of night he lifted up his voice and sang,
Secure, with only two moons listening,
Until the whole harmonious landscape rang—

"For auld lang syne." The weary throat gave out,
The last word wavered; and the song being done,          50
He raised again the jug regretfully
And shook his head, and was again alone.
There was not much that was ahead of him,
And there was nothing in the town below—
Where strangers would have shut the many doors          55
That many friends had opened long ago.


## QUESTIONS

The situation is simple enough. An old man has outlived his time: lines 55–56 tell us that his friends are all dead. His "party" must be with himself, the jug his only companion. He realizes only too well that "most things break" (line 28) and that he is "enduring to the end/A valiant armor of scarred hopes outworn" (lines 17–18). Such a man could be the object of scorn, or derision, or disgust, or pity. Old Eben Flood (what is his name meant to suggest?) comes through the poem as none of these. There is no minimizing of his aloneness, but that aloneness has something of dignity and self-respect in it.

1 ★ Characterize the way Mr. Flood speaks to and answers himself. Is there any self-pity in him? What kind of men might pledge toasts to each other in just this way?

2 ★ What feelings about Mr. Flood do the reference to Roland and his horn call up, here? In what respects is his situation at all like Roland's? In what respects is it not? In what way is his jug like a horn?

3 ★ Is the comparison in lines 25–28 a ridiculous one in this context, or has it been prepared for? (Consider line 14 and the fact that he is already answering himself "huskily.")

4 ★ What action is suggested in lines 31–32 and 36–37? How does it give an added sense of tenderness to his "party"? How do "For auld lang syne" and the "two moons listening" reinforce that sense?

5 ★ Define the tone of the poem.

[9]                     *My Papa's Waltz*
                THEODORE ROETHKE  (1908–1963)

The whiskey on your breath
Could make a small boy dizzy;
But I hung on like death:
Such waltzing was not easy.

We romped until the pans                                    5
Slid from the kitchen shelf;
My mother's countenance
Could not unfrown itself.

The hand that held my wrist
Was battered on one knuckle;                                10
At every step I missed
My right ear scraped a buckle.

You beat time on my head
With a palm caked hard by dirt,
Then waltzed me off to bed                                  15
Still clinging to your shirt.

## QUESTIONS

1 ★ Is the speaker a young boy or a grown man recalling an incident (or
repeated incidents) from childhood? Explain. Who is the audience?
Are there several audiences? Explain.

2 ★ Exactly what is being described? Why is the man "waltzing" his son?
What do lines 3 and 16 tell us about the son's reaction to the "waltz"?
But what does "romped" (line 5) tell us?

3 ★ Explain lines 7–8. Why didn't the mother interfere?

4 ★ The small boy was clearly terrified by the drunken dance. But what
is the grown man's reaction? Consider the title. Consider, too, the use
of "waltzing," "romped," and such a line as "Could not unfrown itself."
How would the implications of the latter differ if it read "Still kept an
icy frown"? In short, how does the tone qualify the sense of terror
remembered?

[ 10 ]                          *Damn Her*

JOHN CIARDI (1916–        )

Of all her appalling virtues, none
leaves more crumbs in my bed, nor
more gravel in my tub
than the hunch of her patience
　　at its mouseholes.                                              5

She would, I swear, outwait
the Sphinx in its homemade quandaries
once any scratching in the walls
has given her to suspect
　　an emergence.                                                  10

It's all in the mind, we say. With her
it's all in the crouch, the waiting
and the doing indistinguishable. Once
she hunches to execution, time is merely
　　the handle of the switch:                                     15

she grasps it and stands by for whatever
will come, certainly, to her sizzling
justice. Then, inevitably always daintily
she closes her total gesture
　　swiftly disdainfully as                                       20

a glutton tosses off a third dozen
oysters—making light of them—as if
his gluttony were a joke that all
may share. The flaps and bellies
　　of his grossness                                              25

are waiting, after all, for something
much more substantial than

appetizers.)—"Bring on the lamb!" her look
says over my empty shells. "Bring on
the body and the blood!" 30

[ 11 ] *Coup de Grâce*

A. D. HOPE (1907–     )

Just at the moment the Wolf,
Shag jaws and slavering grin,
Steps from the property wood,
O, what a gorge, what a gulf
Opens to gobble her in, 5
Little Red Riding Hood!

O, what a face full of fangs!
Eyes like saucers at least
Roll to seduce and beguile.
Miss, with her dimples and bangs, 10
Thinks him a handsome beast;
Flashes the Riding Hood Smile;

Stands her ground like a queen,
Velvet red of the rose
Framing each little milk-tooth, 15
Pink tongue peeping between.
Then, wider than anyone knows,
Opens her minikin mouth

Swallows up Wolf in a trice;
Tail going down gives a flick, 20
Caught as she closes her jaws.
Bows, all sugar and spice.
O, what a lady-like trick!
O, what a round of applause!

QUESTIONS

1 * Each of these poems pays tribute to a woman. What *is* this tribute? How does manipulation of *tone* prevent the tribute from becoming mawkish or sentimental? By what devices is the tone manipulated— allusions? comparisons? word choice? verse form?

2 * Which tribute do you prefer? Why? Do you find the word "tribute" objectionable in this case? Why or why not?

# III
# *THE POEM*
## *AS A*
## *PATTERN OF*
## *RHYTHM AND SOUND*

## Rhythm

### i

All of the aspects of poetry that we have been dealing with thus far apply
as well to literature in prose, although with different emphases. The two
aspects we come to now also have relevance to prose, but it is in this area
of rhythm and sound that the greatest difference lies between poetry and
prose. In a rough kind of way, anyone who has looked at poetry on a page
or who has read some of it aloud is aware that it looks different and reads
differently: it has some kind of definite line and stanza pattern, and some
kind of patterned rhythm or melody.

Line and stanza pattern are obviously peculiar to poetry. Rhythm is
*not*. Everything we say in daily speech has rhythm. In English this rhythm
is dependent mainly on the fact that certain words or syllables get a
heavier stress than do other words or syllables in the stream of speech,
that there are definite rises and falls as the voice moves along, and that
definite kinds of pauses cut up the sound stream, as the following exam-
ples roughly illustrate:

|  |  |
|---|---|
| dóll<br>You need two    ar<br>        s. | Heaviest stress on *doll;* pitch rises on *doll,* then falls and fades, signaling "end of statement." |

73

ars?

dóll

You need two

Heaviest stress on *doll;* pitch rises on *doll,* continues to rise, and fades, signaling "question, please answer."

one, two, three, four, fi

v

e

After each number there is a slight rise in pitch but no voice fade, until the last when pitch falls and voice fades, signaling "end of count."

Smi

t

Mr.     h, my next door

neiǵh         Yańk

bor, likes the     ee

s.

Division indicated by commas in print is signaled in speech by stress and pitch change and voice not fading.

In this discussion we will confine ourselves to stress.[1] Stress is what we hear as loudness or emphasis of a word or syllable in relation to surrounding words or syllables. One-syllable words spoken in isolation—as in the preceding group of numbers or in a list—get what sounds to our ears like equally heavy stress:

**one, two, three, in, hit, walk, four, so, went, five**

In words of two syllables spoken in isolation, one of the syllables gets a heavier stress than the other:

**under, forward, before, sister, arrange, instant, until**

In most two-syllable words, the syllable that does not get heavy stress is sounded weakly, as in the words just cited. But in some two-syllable words, the weaker syllable still gets prominence:

**white**wash, **black**board, **green**house, **moon**lit, **fore**tell

The important point is that the stress is never entirely equal in these cases: the stress on one of the syllables is always slightly heavier. Try pronouncing the foregoing words with major stress on the syllables that are not in

---

[1] What we will say about speech rhythms will be, of necessity, very sketchy. A detailed analysis would have to deal with many other considerations besides stress, but a look at how stress operates gives an adequate introduction to the poet's special way of handling the patterns of language. The discussion is dependent on several suggestions in John Thompson's Introduction to his *The Founding of English Metre* (New York: Columbia University Press, 1961), which, as he says, relies heavily on *An Outline of English Structure,* by George L. Trager and Henry Lee Smith, Jr. (Norman, Okla.: Battenburg Press, 1951).

boldface to see what is meant about unequal stress. Also compare the following pairs to see that there is decided difference in the amount of stress given to the weaker syllables:

> whitewash–whiter
> blackboard–blackness
> greenhouse–greenest
> moonlit–moonlet

In words of more than two syllables, only one of the syllables takes primary or heaviest stress:

benefit, holiday, recovery, transportation, tobacco, intercept, independence, anniversary, constitutional

But differing degrees of weaker stress are likely to fall on the other syllables. For instance, the heaviest stress of "holiday" is on *hol,* but the last syllable, *day,* receives more stress than does the middle syllable, *i.* Similarly, in the last three words listed above, the first syllable does not get primary stress, but gets heavier stress than do the other weak syllables.

In summary, single-syllable words spoken in isolation get definite stress. In two-syllable words, one of the syllables gets major stress and the other gets either almost no stress or an obvious stress weaker than the major one. In words of more than two syllables, one syllable gets primary stress, and the others get almost none or stresses weaker than the primary one. For practice in identifying stress within words, mark the stresses of the following, using ( ' ) for heavy stress, ( ` ) for obvious stress that is not heaviest, and ( ˘ ) for weak stress:

| | | |
|---|---|---|
| fort | accommodate | suburb |
| wigwam | Stonewall | suburban |
| Sunday | automatically | foolhardy |
| formal | sundown | canyon |
| uniform | approach | beginning |
| denounce | wishes | sublet |
| rapid | wishywashy | apprentice |
| fundamental | capital | icebound |

## ii

When words are grouped into phrases, the patterns of heavier and weaker stress depend on the makeup of the word group. For instance, in the phrase "my first anniversary," the heaviest stress normally comes on *ver* (the stressed syllable of the noun that the other words modify), as it does if we pronounce the word in isolation. But if the group is expanded to "my first anniversary party," the heaviest stress normally comes on the first syllable of "party." In the phrase "one small stone," the heaviest stress comes on "stone" if the phrase is spoken normally. (If we deviate from the normal to put heaviest stress on "small," we do it to emphasize a distinction between a small stone and another kind of stone, presumably a larger one. If we deviate from the normal to put the heaviest stress on "one," we do it to emphasize the fact that we are talking about one stone and no more.) If we add the word "house" to the group and get "one small stone house," the heaviest stress now automatically falls on "house," unless, again, we want to make some special distinction.

## iii

Three important observations may now be made. First, as is shown by the shift of heaviest stress to "party" when the word is added to the phrase "my first anniversary" and by the shift of heavier stress to "house" when it is added to "one small stone," heaviest stress in English tends to fall at the end of a word group when the group is spoken normally. Notice the following examples:[1]

a small picket

a small picket fence

a small picket fence gate

running around

running around town

running around Town Hall

---

[1] Most language scholars agree that there are three possible degrees of stress when words are spoken in isolation and four when words are grouped together. Thus, in "my first anniversary party," *par* normally gets heaviest stress, but *first* and *ver* get heavier stress than *my* and *an*, which in turn get heavier stress than the weak-stressed syllables in "anniversary" and "party." It is not easy, without a great deal of training, to decide which of the two medium stresses is present in a given word group. For our purposes, it will be sufficient to distinguish only three degrees of stress within word groups. We will use the symbols designated on page 75.

ăt hĭs báck

ăt hĭs bàck dóor

ăt hĭs bàck dóor wĭndŏw

Thĕ bóy / sànk thrée.

Thĕ smàll bóy / sànk thrèe shíps.

Thĕ smàll bòy pírătĕ / sànk thrèe shìps éasĭlў.

Second, some classes of words automatically get weaker or stronger stress because of what they are. Any *preposition* ("in," "on," "with"), any *noun marker* ("a," "an," "the," "every"), any *auxiliary* ("is," "will be," "has been," plus a verb), most *pronouns* ("he," "his," "it"), and any simple *conjunction* ("and," "but," "so") normally get weak stress. Nouns in their normal positions usually get primary stress: subject—"The *boy* is awake"; direct object—"We buried the *cat*"; and object of preposition—"on the *beach*". Modifiers that precede the word they modify normally get medium stress:

smàll grèen búsh

crùmblĭng stòne wáll

quìet ăntìcĭpátĭon

quìetlў thínkĭng

Predicate adjectives ("She seemed *sick*"; "He's *healthy*") and adverbs in final sentence position ("He caught the ball *easily*"; "Your check came *through*") normally take primary stress. Verbs as predicates seldom get heaviest stress, unless they appear at the end of a sentence:

Hĕ càlled thĕ dóg.

Thĕ sún sànk dòwn ĭn thĕ wést.

Wĕ sàt quíetlў.

Thĕy léft.

Third, what these two facts about English mean in practice is that we may have an extraordinary variety of speech rhythms in ordinary, every-

day word groups. We encounter groups in which every word receives
some appreciable stress:

> old gray stone wall
>
> sank coal crates there
>
> Please leave coats here.
>
> Young dogs bark loud.

We encounter groups in which weakly stressed and strongly stressed
words and syllables alternate to make remarkably regular patterns:

> the house of stone in Bangor, Maine
>
> my friend who thinks he's Cary Grant
>
> All of the hoods will be whooping it up in the spring.

We even encounter groups whose patterns of regularity are so prolonged
that they can be turned into a crude form of versification with minimal
effort. Consider the following sentence quoted from *The Founding of
English Metre*, mentioned earlier: "What metre adds to language is pre-
cisely the element of imitation that makes of the two, when they are
joined, the art of verse." If we eliminate the words "the element of" and
emphasize the particular phrasing we want by printing the passage in
lines, we get a clumsy stanza:

> What metre adds to language is
> Precisely imitation,
> That makes of the two, when they are joined,
> The art of vers[ification].

The result is far from poetry, but it shows how easily speech patterns may
be directed toward the regularities and semiregularities that we call the
meters of verse.

## iv

The poet is a man who pays attention to the facts about speech that we
have been discussing and makes it his business to arrange words so that
their speech rhythms will accomplish something. The two things normally

accomplished are (1) the heightening of pleasure—because we all enjoy rhythm—and (2) the heightening or clarification of meaning. Let us look at an instance of the latter first, in a short poem titled "The Span of Life":

> The old dog barks backward without getting up.
> I can remember when he was a pup.
>
> —*The Span of Life*
> ROBERT FROST (1874–1963)

In this short poem, the old dog is contrasted with the pup he once was. The words of the first line describe his behavior now; the words of the second line, notably the word "pup," refer to him as he was then. This contrast in what the lines say is paralleled in the respective rhythms. The first line contains relatively heavy stresses bunched together:

The old dog barks backward without getting up.

Speaking playfully, we might say that the line, like the dog, refuses to get up off its haunches and move. Speaking more exactly, we can at least say that the line is heavy and halting in a way that suits the idea of an old dog not wanting to get up. The second line, on the other hand, has a swift, light, and fairly regular movement:

I can remember when he was a pup.

Its movement is lively—like the pup's, we might say if speaking playfully, but at any rate lively in a manner that fits the idea of a capering young dog. And here there is a further point to notice. Though some sort of contrasting relation is established between the old dog and the young one by what the words say, we do not know precisely what the contrast is until we pay attention to the rhythm. So far as the words are concerned, the point might be that the old dog is no longer so good a watchdog as he was. It is the contrast in the rhythms that helps direct our attention to the differing movements of the two ages of dog, and so helps us to understand that the young one is all curiosity, barking at everything it sees, and rushing to see everything it barks at, while the old one, having been through all this, simply turns his head and *barks backward*.

## QUESTIONS

Where in the following passages would you say that rhythm *most clearly* heightens or clarifies meaning?

1 ★ Here is a Greek warrior at the siege of Troy struggling to hurl a great boulder against his Trojan enemies:

> When Ajax strives some rock's vast weight to throw,
> The line too labors, and the words move slow.

—From *An Essay on Criticism*
ALEXANDER POPE (1688–1744)

2 ★ Here is a thirsty man in a desert, longing for water. (The cicada he speaks of is the grasshopper locust.)

> If there were the sound of water only
> Not the cicada
> And dry grass singing
> But sound of water over a rock
> Where the hermit-thrush sings in the pine trees                    5
> Drip drop drip drop drop drop drop
> But there is no water

—From *The Waste Land,* V
T. S. ELIOT (1888–1965)

3 ★ Here is a complete poem called "Reflections on Ice-Breaking":

> Candy
> Is dandy
> But liquor
> Is quicker.

—*Reflections on Ice-Breaking*
OGDEN NASH (1902–1971)

To appreciate the part played by rhythm in the previous example, notice what rephrasing the poem does:

> In my experience I have found that candy
> For purposes of social ice-breaking is dandy,
> But if I had to choose, I think I'd choose liquor,
> As being on the whole and in most circumstances quicker.

4 ★ Here is a knight in his armor ("harness") clambering among rocks in a mighty effort to reach a lake before the wounded man he carries on his back dies:

Dry clashed his harness in the icy caves
And barren chasms, and all to left and right
The bare black cliff clanged round him, as he based
His feet on juts of slippery crag that rang
Sharp-smitten with the dint of armèd heels—     5
And on a sudden, lo! the level lake,
And the long glories of the winter moon.

—From *Morte d'Arthur*
ALFRED, LORD TENNYSON (1809–1892)

5 ★ Here is a description of a crowded three-lane expressway at the height
of the evening rush hour, the lanes of traffic moving at high speed:

Evening traffic homeward burns,
Swift and even on the turns,
Drifting weight in triple rows,
Fixed relation and repose.
This one edges out and by,     5
Inch by inch with steady eye.
But should error be increased,
Mass and moment are released;
Matter loosens, flooding blind,
Levels driver to its kind.     10

—From *Before Disaster*
YVOR WINTERS (1900–     )

6 ★ Here is a story of a man who gets hanged just as the poem, titled
"Eight O'Clock," ends. How does the language of the last two lines imi-
tate the actions of the clock before striking and the action of the trap
door through which the condemned man plunges?

He stood, and heard the steeple
    Sprinkle the quarters on the morning town.
One, two, three, four, to market place and people
    It tossed them down.

Strapped, noosed, nighing his hour,     5
    He stood and counted them and cursed his luck.
And then the clock collected in the tower
    Its strength, and struck.

—*Eight O'Clock*
A. E. HOUSMAN (1859–1936)

What would be lost if the second stanza were as follows?

> Unable to move, awaiting his time,
> He stood and counted them and cursed his luck.
> Then, in the tower, the clock did chime,
> Sealing his doom when it struck.

7 ★ Here is a poem about a decision. The finality of decision is hammered home by line length and rhythm. Notice the abrupt second and fourth lines of the first two stanzas and the even more abrupt second and fourth lines in the last stanza, giving the effect of firmness and fixity.

> The soul selects her own society,
> Then shuts the door;
> On her divine majority
> Obtrude no more.
>
> Unmoved, she notes the chariot's pausing         5
> At her low gate;
> Unmoved, an emperor is kneeling
> Upon her mat.
>
> I've known her from an ample nation
> Choose one;         10
> Then close the valves of her attention
> Like stone.

> —*The Soul Selects Her Own Society*
> EMILY DICKINSON (1830–1886)

## Meter

### i

From the preceding examples we can see that rhythm may support and clarify meaning. But rhythm may also please for its own sake, and the principle that accounts for the pleasure it gives is the principle of recurrence with change.

Our lives are rooted in things that recur: the four seasons, day and night, our three meals a day, work and relaxation, breathing, blinking, and a thousand more. We find something secure and satisfying in old friends, old tunes, old slippers, old scenes. At the same time, however, we long for variety. We like to see new faces as well as old ones, eat new foods in new places, move through a variety of responsibilities in our jobs. Many of the things that especially delight us therefore are those in which a strong element of recurrence is balanced by a strong element of change. From this combination comes much of the appeal of music and dancing (for these are built of stated themes and fixed steps opening out into variations and improvisations)—and the appeal of poetry.

Regular rhythmic recurrence in poetry is called *meter*. The recurrence is essentially a stress recurrence, or, more accurately, a "weak-stress–strong-stress" recurrence. The normal stress pattern of speech is fitted into a two-stress metrical pattern, having (in most English poetry) the major stress second. In the examples, we will use *o* to mark *metric* weak stresses and *s* to mark metric strong stresses to keep clear the distinction between *metrical* stress patterns and *speech* stress patterns.

$$o \quad s \quad\quad o \quad s \quad\quad o \quad s$$
**weak-strong, weak-strong, weak-strong**

or

$$o \; s \quad\quad o \; s \quad\quad o \; s$$
**ta-tum, ta-tum, ta-tum**

or

$$o \quad s \quad o \quad s \quad o \quad s$$
to **barn** and **stack** and **tree**

When the speech stresses are subjected to the two-stress metrical pattern, primary speech stresses generally remain strong and weak speech stresses generally remain weak. Medium speech stresses become metric strongs or metric weaks depending on the surrounding stresses; between strong or medium stresses they become metric weaks, and between weak stresses they become metric strongs. Also, weak speech stresses sometimes become strong metric stresses when they come between two weak speech stresses that are also weak metric stresses. Thus in any given line of verse, single-syllable words can have stresses not normally received in speech. Obviously, however, the unstressed syllables of multisyllable words cannot take strong metric stresses if the result would be an incorrect pronunciation of the word. Likewise, insistence on giving equal emphasis to all strong metric stresses in defiance of normal speech rhythms creates distortion.

A few examples will make clear what we have been saying. Let us look at the first stanza of "The Man He Killed" (p. 31), marked first with normal speech stresses:

Had he and I but met

By some old ancient inn,

We should have sat us down to wet

Right many a nipperkin!

The first line clearly indicates the weak-strong pattern in normal speech and sets the metrical pattern by which the second line is read. As is clear, the "metric-weak–metric-strong" movement suggested in the first line accommodates the language of the second line very effectively. The normally weak-stressed "by" and the normal pronunciation of "ancient inn" provide the framework; "old" gets weak metric stress coming between the relative strongs on "some" and the first syllable of "ancient." If, however, the words "In the dark alley near the warehouse" followed "Had he and I but met," the potential pattern established in the first six words would be effectively annulled, and we would probably ignore the regularity of the first line. Even when the substitute second line is printed in verse form, it does not give us a suggestion of metric regularity:

> Had he and I but met
> In the dark alley near the warehouse . . .

On the other hand, in Hardy's lines printed as prose the regularity remains:

> Had he and I but met by some old ancient inn . . .

The third line of the stanza fits smoothly, with the established metrical pattern hinting a strong on "should" and a weak on "we." The speech rhythm of the last line also fits the metrical pattern, with the almost unnoticeable addition of two weak stresses in a row: "many a." (But we may see how effective the slight break in the established pattern is by contrasting the present line with the more metrically regular "So many nipperkins!")

Now let us mark the second stanza of Hardy's poem with metric strongs and weaks instead of speech rhythm stresses:

> o    s   o  s o  s
> But ranged as infantry,
> o    s   o    s  o    s
> And staring face to face,
> o  s   o   s   o  s o  s
> I shot at him as he at me,
> o   s   o  s o   s
> And killed him in his place.

The strong metric stresses and the strong speech stresses match almost perfectly, the only marked deviation coming in the last line where the weak speech stress on "in" gets strong metric stress, coming as it does between two weak speech stresses. This is not to say that "in" should be given much more emphasis than it would normally have in speech. To emphasize it results in an unnatural singsong. On the other hand, the listener or reader must be aware that the metrical stress falls where it does, and the line should not be read as if it were part of a prose sentence, such as, "When he reappeared near the battered tank, I took careful aim and killed him in his place."

## ii

We have noted previously that the "weak-strong" metric pattern is dominant in English poetry. This metric pattern is called *iambic*, and its individual units are called *iambs*, or sometimes (since a basic unit of measurement in English meter is the *foot*, formed in this case of one weak stress and one strong stress) *iambic feet*. Almost every poem we have looked at thus far is in the iambic pattern. Here are some examples. Read them aloud—but do not fail to remember that when a weak speech stress and a strong metric stress, or a strong speech stress and a weak metric stress, fall on the same syllable or word, the speech stresses are only slightly modified: the weak speech stress in a strong metric position will take a very *little* more emphasis than it would normally have, and the strong speech stress in a weak metric position will take a very *little* less emphasis.

 s     o     o   s  o    s    o  s   o    s
Something there is that doesn't love a wall,
 o    s    o    s    o        s    o   s   o  s
That sends the frozen-ground-swell under it,
 o    s     o   s   o     s    o   s   o     s
And spills the upper boulders in the sun; . . .

—From *Mending Wall* (p. 8)

 o     s      o   s     o   s   o    s   o    s
Cliff Klingenhagen had me in to dine
 o    s    o    s    o   s  o   s   o     s
With him one day; and after soup and meat,
 o    s   o    s    o     s   o    s   o    s
And all the other things there were to eat, . . .

—From *Cliff Klingenhagen* (p. 10)

 o   s     o    s     o    s   o
In summertime on Bredon
   o    s    o    s    o    s
The bells they sound so clear; . . .

—From *Bredon Hill* (p. 11)

     s   o    o     s      o    s     o     s
Brushing from whom the stiffened puke
o   s    o    s  o s  o   s
i put him all into my arms
o     s     o     s      o    s   o    s
and staggered banged with terror through
o     s   o    s  o    s  o    s
a million billion trillion stars.

—From *A Man Who Had Fallen Among Thieves* (*p. 15*)

o    s    o s  o s  o    s
A sweet disorder in the dress
s   o   o    s     o    s   o    s
Kindles in clothes a wantonness; . . .

—From *Delight in Disorder* (*p. 19*)

o   s   o    s  o   s   o     s
A narrow fellow in the grass
o   s  o s o   s
Occasionally rides;
o    s    o    s   o     s  o    s
You may have met him,—did you not?
o    s    o    s   o    s
His notice sudden is.

—From *A Narrow Fellow in the Grass* (*p. 21*)

This iambic (weak-strong) meter dominates English poetry because it is a regularization of the basic rhythmic pattern of the language itself. English sentences are built as a series of word groups; and, as we have seen, the stress pattern of the word group is essentially weak-strong, since the primary stress almost always comes at the end of the group. The imposed iambic meter is thus a "model of the larger units of the language"[1] itself, or as the quotation used earlier puts it: "What metre adds to language is precisely the element of imitation that makes of the two, when they are joined, the art of verse."[2] We have, therefore, in any line of verse two separate rhythmic considerations to combine into a third:

1. The two-stress metrical pattern.
2. The normal speech rhythm stress.
3. The actual product of these two in any given line.

---

[1] John Thompson, *The Founding of English Metre* (New York: Columbia University Press, 1961), p. 12.

[2] *Ibid.*, p. 9.

Since there are always weak and strong stresses at work in metered English poetry, there can be other ways of ordering them than the iambic pattern. It is simplest, and also most accurate, to think of these other patterns as variations on the iambic, and that is how we shall treat them here. The most obvious variation comes from reversing the iamb to produce a "strong-weak" meter. The individual unit, or foot, is called in this case a *trochee,* and the over-all pattern or meter is called *trochaic.* Here is a good specimen of it in a stanza from Tennyson's "The Lady of Shalott":

s   o   s   o   s o   s   o
Willows whiten, aspens quiver,

s   o   s   o   s   o   s   o
Little breezes dusk and shiver

s      o   s      o   s   o s o
Through the wave that runs forever

s   o   s   o   s   o   s o
By the island in the river

s   o   s   o   s o s
Flowing down to Camelot.                              5

s   o   s      o   s   o   s   o
Four gray walls, and four gray towers,

s   o s   o   s   o   s   o
Overlook a space of flowers,

s   o   s   o   s   o   s   o
And the silent isle imbowers

o   s   o s o   s
The Lady of Shalott.

Very few poems in English are written in this consistently trochaic meter. Many, however, are written with four strong metric stresses in each line, with one of the strongs at the beginning and one at the end, as in the following:

s   o   s o   s      o      s
Evening traffic homeward burns,

s   o s   o   s   o   s
Swift and even on the turns,

s   o   s   o   s o   s
Drifting weight in triple rows,

s   o s o   s   o s
Fixed relation and repose.

—From *Before Disaster*
YVOR WINTERS (1900–     )

s   o   s   o   s   o      s
Earth, receive an honored guest;

s   o   s   o   s   o   s
William Yeats is laid to rest:

s   o  s o   s  o  s
Let the Irish vessel lie
s   o   s   o  s o s
Emptied of its poetry.

—From *In Memory of W. B. Yeats*
W. H. AUDEN (1907–   )

s   o   s   o   s   o     s
Tiger, Tiger, burning bright
s   o   s   o   s   o    s
In the forests of the night,
s    o   s   o    s   o  s
What immortal hand or eye
o    s   o   s o   s   o s
Could frame thy fearful symmetry?

—From *The Tiger*
WILLIAM BLAKE (1757–1827)

Such meters are best looked on as essentially iambic despite the strong opening stresses in each line. We might, of course, regard them as imperfectly trochaic—but notice the damage done by the weak final syllable when we recast into perfect trochaic:

s   o    s  o   s     o    s   o
Evening traffic homeward burning,
Swift and even on the turning,
Drifting weight in go condition,
Fixed in triple-laned position.

s    o   s    o  s    o     s  o
Earth, receive an honored patron;
William Yeats has changed his matron:
See the Irish vessel lying
Emptied of its versifying.

s    o  s   o   s   o    s   o
Tiger, Tiger, burning brightly
In the forest darkness nightly.

There is much less damage when we recast, instead, to supply the weak first syllable of perfect iambic:

o    s   o    s  o    s   o    s
As evening traffic homeward burns,
It's swift and even on the turns,
All drifting weight in triple rows,
In fixed relation and repose.

Sweet Earth, receive an honored guest;
Our William Yeats is laid to rest:
O let the Irish vessel lie
Now emptied of its poetry.

O Tiger, Tiger, burning bright
In all the forests of the night.

Opening and closing with a strong stress, the original lines have maximum weight for their length.

A second major variation on iambic is the *anapest* or *anapestic foot*, a pattern of two metrically unstressed words or syllables followed by a stressed one. This foot is essentially an iamb with an extra metric weak inserted before the metric strong:

With a leap and a bound the swift anapests throng.

SAMUEL TAYLOR COLERIDGE (1772–1834)

As a sloop with a sweep of immaculate wings on her delicate spine
And a keel as steel as a root that holds in the sea as she leans,

—From Buick<br>KARL SHAPIRO (1913–    )

"Oh where are you going?" said reader to rider,
"The valley is fatal when furnaces burn,
Yonder's the midden whose odors will madden,
That gap is the grave where the tall return."

—From O Where Are You Going?<br>W. H. AUDEN (1907–    )

I sprang to the stirrup, and Joris, and he;
I galloped, Dirck galloped, we galloped all three;
"Good speed!" cried the watch, as the gatebolts undrew;
"Speed!" echoed the wall to us galloping through;

—From How They Brought the Good News from Ghent to Aix<br>ROBERT BROWNING (1812–1889)

It is obvious from the examples given that a poem dominated by anapestic meter in English has a "leap and a bound," as Coleridge says, or at least a sense of swift movement that is not congenial to very many subjects. The same observation is true of the third variation, the *dactyl*. This is a strong metric stress followed by two weak metric stresses —in other words, a trochee with an extra metric weak inserted after the metric strong, as in the following:

Take her up tenderly,

Lift her with care,

Fashioned so slenderly,

Young, and so fair!

—From *The Bridge of Sighs*
THOMAS HOOD (1799–1845)

Though they occur with some frequency as variations within iambic lines, both anapestic and dactylic meters have very limited use in English. As we have noted, they are used as basic meters mainly for special subjects, as in Shapiro's "Buick." The fact is that any *sustained* deviations from iambic meter call attention to themselves so pointedly (with exceptions that we shall discuss later) that under most circumstances the deviations would put undue emphasis on form at the expense of meaning.

One other kind of metrical variation should be mentioned: the recurrence of several strong-stressed syllables in a row. Since regular speech rhythms must receive their due in poetry, there are bound to be cases where several such stresses succeed each other, as we saw in "The Span of Life" (p. 79). The following examples illustrate gradations of this kind of variation. The first three contain obviously strong stresses with definite pauses between them; the second three have stress strong enough to override the regular meter and therefore to slow down the movement of the line considerably; the third three get definite speech rhythm stress, but not enough to force strong metric stress:

**Blow, blow,** ye wintry winds . . .

**Break, break, break,**
    On thy cold gray stones, O sea! . . .

**Out, out,** brief candle . . .

When Ajax strives some **rock's vast weight** to throw  . . .

The apparition of these faces in a crowd:
Petals on a **wet, black bough.**

The old **dog barks back**ward without getting up, . . .

By **some old** ancient inn. . . .

And Camelot, and **starlit Stonehenge.**

Mine, O thou lord of life, **send my roots rain.**

### iii

We come back now to the way in which speech stress and metrical stress come together to form poetic rhythm—the actual rhythm of the verse line. Left to itself with no counterforce against it, regular metrical recurrence, even with occasional substitution of the kind we have just looked at, would produce results like this:

She SHOULD have DIED here AF ter;
There WOULD have BEEN a TIME for SUCH a WORD.
To MOR row, AND to MOR row, AND to MOR row,
Creeps IN this PET ty PACE from DAY to DAY,
To THE last SYL la BLE of re COR ded TIME;                    5
And ALL our YES ter DAYS have LIGHT ed FOOLS
The WAY to DUST y DEATH. Out, OUT, brief CAN dle!
Life's BUT a WALK ing SHAD ow, A poor PLAY er
That STRUTS and FRETS his HOUR up ON the STAGE
And THEN is HEARD no MORE. It IS a TALE                       10
Told BY an ID iot, FULL of SOUND and FU ry,
Sig NIF (y)ing NOTH ing.

—From *Macbeth,* V, v
WILLIAM SHAKESPEARE (1564–1616)

But speech rhythm supplies that counterforce, creating in the line a sort of tug-of-war, or tension, that brings pleasure to the tongue and ear. If we read the *Macbeth* passage, taking account of its speech rhythms as well as its meter, we get:

She should have died here af ter;

There would have been a time for such a word.

To mor row, and to mor row, and to mor row,

Creeps in this pet ty pace from day to day,

To the last syl la ble of re cor ded time;                    5

And all our yes ter days have light ed fools

The way to dust y death. Out, out, brief can dle!

Life's but a walk ing shad ow, a poor play er

That struts and frets his hour u pon the stage

And then is heard no more. It is a tale                       10

Told by an id iot, full of sound and fur y,

Sig ni fy ing noth ing.

Read in this way the varying speech rhythms pull against the implied fixed meter, but are never allowed to destroy it. Just the opposite, in fact: a more than usual divergence from regularity, as in lines 7–8, is likely to be compensated by a more than usual regularity, as in lines 9–10.

Now notice how in E. A. Robinson's "Cliff Klingenhagen" the speech stresses of the first three lines match almost perfectly the metrical stresses, primarily because the weak-stressed words and syllables match the weak metric stresses. Then, in the fourth line come four definite speech stresses in a row that slow down the smooth flow of the first three lines and in a sense "act out" the deliberateness with which Cliff Klingenhagen serves the wine and wormwood. The metrical stress is marked above the speech stress.

o   s  o s o   s   o  s o   s
Cliff Klingenhagen had me in to dine

o    s   o   s  o   s   o      s
With him one day; and after soup and meat,

o   s   o   s o   s     o   s   o s
And all the other things there were to eat,

o   s   o   s  o
Cliff took two glasses . . .

For further illustration of the rhythmic variation that the marriage of metrical pattern and speech rhythm produces, look at the following first lines of poems, all of which are in the same metrical pattern (five iambs to each line):

Cliff Klingenhagen had me in to dine . . .

When I see birches bend to left and right . . .

When I have fears that I may cease to be . . .

Thou art indeed just, Lord, if I contend . . .

To be, or not to be—that is the question . . .

Avenge, O Lord, thy slaughtered saints, whose bones . . .

Five years have passed; five summers, with the length . . .

There was a time when meadow, grove, and stream . . .

The same kind of wide variation may be seen in the following lines, all of which are iambic with four strong poetic stresses:

It is an ancient mariner . . .

She walks in beauty, like the night . . .

Earth, receive an honored guest . . .

Stern Daughter of the Voice of God . . .

Behold her, single in the field . . .

Mock on, mock on, Voltaire, Rousseau . . .

Love seeketh not itself to please . . .

The morning comes to consciousness . . .

To summarize, poetic rhythm combines regularity with irregularity. Regularity most often is the result of some definite underlying meter. Irregularity comes mainly from normal speech rhythms. There is no hard and fast line between the two. When we have speech rhythms free from any obvious pattern of recurrence, we have prose. When we have unrelieved regularity of metrical pattern, we have a singsong. Pleasurable poetic rhythms remain far removed from either extreme.

## iv

We can now look at other factors that have a great deal to do with determining regularity and irregularity in a poem: line length, stanza pattern, and the speech sounds themselves.

*Line length* is a matter of the number of individual units, or feet, that succeed each other in the line. It is not impossible to have lines of one foot or even six feet, but these are rare in English verse. Most lines have three feet (trimeter), four feet (tetrameter), or five feet (pentameter).

*Stanza pattern* is determined by the length of the line and the patterning of the rhyme scheme. A stanza like those in Emily Dickinson's "Apparently with No Surprise" (p. 61) contains alternate lines of four feet and three—usually represented for brevity's sake as 4, 3, 4, 3. Its rhymes (if we accept the "eye-rhyme" of the second stanza) occur at the end of the second and fourth lines in each stanza—usually represented as a, b, c, b. A stanza like that of Leigh Hunt's "The Nun" (p. 60) has lines of three feet, except for line 8, which has four. This pattern is represented 3, 3, 3, 3, 3, 3, 3, 4, 3. Its rhymes link the first and third lines, the second and fourth lines, the fifth and sixth lines, and the seventh and ninth lines; the eighth line is unrhymed. This pattern is represented a, b, a, b, c, c, d, e, d.

The following passages give you a chance to test your ability to recognize line lengths and stanza patterns. Read the passages aloud and then answer the questions at the close.

[1]              From *King Richard II*, III, ii
              WILLIAM SHAKESPEARE (1564–1616)

    For God's sake, let us sit upon the ground
    And tell sad stories of the death of kings:
    How some have been deposed; some slain in war;
    Some haunted by the ghosts they have deposed;
    Some poisoned by their wives; some sleeping killed;      5
    All murdered:

[2]              From *To His Coy Mistress*
              ANDREW MARVELL (1621–1678)

    But at my back I always hear
    Time's wingèd chariot hurrying near.

[3]    From *Elegy Written in a Country Churchyard*
        THOMAS GRAY (1716–1771)

>   The curfew tolls the knell of parting day,
>   The lowing herd wind slowly o'er the lea,
>   The plowman homeward plods his weary way,
>   And leaves the world to darkness and to me.

[4]    From *She Dwelt Among the Untrodden Ways*
        WILLIAM WORDSWORTH (1770–1850)

>   She dwelt among the untrodden ways
>       Beside the springs of Dove,
>   A maid whom there were none to praise,
>       And very few to love.

[5]    From *Antony and Cleopatra,* IV, xiv
        WILLIAM SHAKESPEARE (1564–1616)

>           I, that with my sword
>   Quartered the world, and o'er green Neptune's back
>   With ships made cities, condemn myself to lack
>   The courage of a woman; less noble mind
>   Than she which by her death our Caesar tells,     5
>   "I am conqueror of myself."

[6]                    From *Satire III*
                JOHN DONNE (1572–1631)

>           On a high hill,
>   Ragged and steep, Truth dwells, and he that will
>   Reach her, about must, and about must go;
>   And what the hill's suddenness resists, win so.

[7]                    From *To Autumn*

JOHN KEATS (1795–1821)

Season of mists and mellow fruitfulness,
    Close bosom-friend of the maturing sun;
Conspiring with him how to load and bless
    With fruit the vines that round the thatch-eaves run.

[8]              From *The Wild Swans at Coole*

WILLIAM BUTLER YEATS (1865–1939)

The trees are in their autumn beauty,
The woodland paths are dry,
Under the October twilight the water
Mirrors a still sky;
Upon the brimming water among the stones          5
Are nine-and-fifty swans.

[9]                  From *My Papa's Waltz*

THEODORE ROETHKE (1908–1963)

The whiskey on your breath
Could make a small boy dizzy;
But I held on like death:
Such waltzing was not easy.

[10]                    From *Preludes*

T. S. ELIOT (1888–1965)

The morning comes to consciousness
Of faint stale smells of beer
From the sawdust-trampled street
With all its muddy feet that press

To early coffee-stands.                                              5
With the other masquerades
That time resumes,
One thinks of all the hands
That are raising dingy shades
In a thousand furnished rooms.                                      10


## QUESTIONS

1 ⋆ Which of these passages would you put toward the end of the spec-
trum where speech rhythms run most completely parallel to meter?
Which toward the end where regular meter is most submerged by
speech rhythms? Which more or less in the middle?

2 ⋆ Represent the line lengths in each passage and the rhyme scheme of
each that has one.

3 ⋆ Indicate the places in each of the selections where the basic iambic
meter has been replaced by a variation. Give particular attention to
the questions below:

  a. In passage 2 how does the variation in the second line match the
  line's movement to its meaning? Consider as an alternative:

      Time's wingèd carriage hasting near.

  b. In passage 5 what is the effect of the heavy stress at the beginning
  of line 2 (with the vowel sound of "sword" repeated)? Consider
  the alternative:

          I, that with my sword
      Have fourthed the world . . .

  In the same passage, what would be lost if the last two lines read:

      Than she which by her death our Caesar tells
      That she is master of herself.

  c. In passage 6 how does the rhythm support the meaning of the
  lines? What is the effect of ending the second line on "will"?
  Would the word get stress otherwise? Why should it? What is
  gained by repeating "about must"? How does "must" get promi-
  nence? Why should it? What does "suddenness" mean in this con-

text? How is "suddenness" emphasized? What is the purpose of setting the last two short words off as they are? Which word gets heaviest stress? Perhaps a revision will throw light on the original by comparison:

> On a mighty hill,
> Ragged and steep, dwells Truth, and he
> That will reach her, about must go,
> And what the hill's surprise resists, win so.

What is lost in the revision?

d. In passage 10 what is the effect of the extra foot in line 4? (The reader expects a three-foot line, especially when he reaches "feet" to rhyme with "street," but he is made to go on to "press.") How does this extra foot emphasize "press" and why does Eliot want it emphasized? The speech stresses and the metric stresses of the last three lines are almost identical, the only difference being that line 8 begins with one unstressed word, while 9 and 10 begin with two. Mark the speech stresses of the last three lines. How does the repeated pattern match the meaning of the lines? ("Hands" are "raising . . . shades" in a "thousand . . . rooms.")

## V

Two other kinds of rhythm patterns we have not dealt with yet. One is called *strong-stress meter*. Here the rhythm of the line is dependent on four strong metric stresses with no set number of metric weak stresses between them. There is usually a pause or split in the middle of such lines. The lines are usually end-stopped (that is, the sense does not run unbrokenly over the line end, as it does in line 3 of passage 8 above). The stresses are usually underscored by a repetition of sounds (usually consonant sounds), as in the following:

> This is a wild land, country of my choice,
>   With harsh craggy mountain, moor ample and bare.
> Seldom in these acres is heard any voice
>   But voice of cold water that runs here and there
>   Through rocks and lank heather growing without care.     5
> No mice in the heath run nor no birds cry
> For fear of the dark speck that floats in the sky.

> —From *Rocky Acres*
> ROBERT GRAVES (1895–

The difference between these lines and more normally metrical lines can be seen if the stanza is written metrically (which at once destroys much of its effectiveness):

> This land is very wild, this land that is my choice,
>     With harsh and craggy mountains, vast and cold and bare.
> Seldom in these acres is heard any voice
>     But voice of icy water running here and there
>         Through rocks and heather lank and past the foxes' lair.      5
> No mice will run in the heath and birds will never cry
> For fear of all the dark specks that float up in the sky.

Since in strong-stress meter the number of unstressed syllables is relatively unimportant, it does not make much sense to talk about its metrical feet, even though many lines can be analyzed in terms of the kinds of meters we have been discussing. The important thing is to give all the stresses their due—to emphasize the stress pattern created. Read the following four lines and try to decide where the strong stresses fall:

> The world is charged with the grandeur of God.
>     It will flame out, like shining from shook foil;
>     It gathers to a greatness, like the ooze of oil
> Crushed. Why do men then now not reck his rod?

> —From *God's Grandeur*
>     GERARD MANLEY HOPKINS (1844–1889)

The dominance of the strong stresses in this kind of meter can be seen if we rewrite the lines, adding eight extra syllables:

> The heavens are gloried with the grandeur of God.
>     It will flame outward, like the shining from shaken foil;
>     It will gather to a greatness, like the oozing of oil
> Crushed. Why do men then now not reckon with his rod?

We do not say that the additions leave the rhythm of Hopkins's poem unmarred, but simply that the strong-stress pattern is so powerful rhythmically that the added syllables can not altogether destroy it or submerge it. If eight syllables were thus added to four lines of iambic meter, there would be no rhythm left.

Before discussing what is called "free verse," a third major kind of rhythmic structure, let us look at a few more examples of strong-stress meter. The first two are so regular that they can as well be considered conventionally metered. In like manner, Auden's "O Where Are You Going?" (p. 108) can be considered strong-stressed as well as anapestic.

> Where the gray seas glitter and the sharp tides shift,
> And the sea-folk labor and the red sails lift.

> —From *Lepanto*
> GILBERT KEITH CHESTERTON (1874–1936)

> Till the slow sea rise and the sheer cliff crumble,
> Till terrace and meadow the deep gulfs drink,
> Till the strength of the waves of the high tides humble
> The fields that lessen, the rocks that shrink, . . .

> —From *A Forsaken Garden*
> ALGERNON CHARLES SWINBURNE (1837–1909)

In many modern poems the rhythmic structure is a mixture of conventional meters and strong-stress meter. See how well you can distinguish the ingredients of this mixture in the following examples:

> Phlebas the Phoenician, a fortnight dead,
> Forgot the cry of gulls, and the deep sea swell
> And the profit and loss.
> A current under sea
> Picked his bones in whispers. As he rose and fell          5
> He passed the stages of his age and youth
> Entering the whirlpool.
> Gentile or Jew
> O you who turn the wheel and look to windward,
> Consider Phlebas, who was once handsome and tall as you.          10

> —From *The Waste Land, IV*
> T. S. ELIOT (1888–1965)

> There head falls forward, fatigued at evening,
> And dreams of home,
> Waving from window, spread of welcome,
> Kissing of wife under single sheet;
> But waking sees          5
> Bird-flocks nameless to him, through doorway voices
> Of new men making another love.

> —From *Something Is Bound to Happen*
> W. H. AUDEN (1907–     )

Deep with the first dead lies London's daughter,
Robed in the long friends,
The grains beyond age, the dark veins of her mother
Secret by the unmourning water
Of the riding Thames.                                    5
After the first death, there is no other.

—From *A Refusal to Mourn the Death,
by Fire, of a Child in London*
DYLAN THOMAS (1914–1953)


## vi

"Free verse" is not verse in the sense in which we have been using the term so far. It would be better to call it a poetic rhythm free *from* verse —free from any kind of definite metrical pattern, although any free verse poem has occasional lines and phrases with obvious metrical regularity.

Yet there is pattern in free verse, and it is achieved in a number of ways: through the repetition of sounds, words, and grammatical structures; through the paralleling of ideas; even through the use of special printing effects on the page, as in "plato told him" (p. 27). Some very subtle rhythms have been achieved in free verse poems, as should be clear from the following examples.


[11]                    *Twenty-third Psalm*

KING JAMES VERSION

The Lord is my shepherd; I shall not want.
He maketh me to lie down in green pastures;
He leadeth me beside the still waters;
He restoreth my soul;
He leadeth me in the paths of righteousness for His name's sake.    5
Yea, though I walk through the valley of the shadow of death,
I will fear no evil: for Thou art with me;
Thy rod and Thy staff they comfort me.
Thou preparest a table before me in the presence of mine enemies:
Thou anointest my head with oil; my cup runneth over.               10
Surely goodness and mercy shall follow me all the days of my life.
And I shall dwell in the house of the Lord forever.

[12]     *When I Heard the Learn'd Astronomer*
                WALT WHITMAN (1819–1892)

When I heard the learn'd astronomer,
When the proofs, the figures, were ranged in columns before me,
When I was shown the charts and diagrams, to add, divide, and
     measure them,
When I sitting heard the astronomer where he lectured with much
     applause in the lecture room,
How soon unaccountable I became tired and sick,                    5
Till rising and gliding out I wander'd off by myself,
In the mystical moist night-air, and from time to time,
Look'd up in perfect silence at the stars.


[13]           From *Snake*
                D. H. LAWRENCE (1885–1930)

He lifted his head from his drinking, as cattle do,
And looked at me vaguely, as drinking cattle do,
And flickered his two-forked tongue from his lips, and mused a
     moment,
And stooped and drank a little more,
Being earth brown, earth golden from the burning burning bowels
     of the earth                                                  5
On the day of Sicilian July, with Etna smoking.


QUESTIONS

1 ★ In poems 11 and 12 what kinds of repetition give a sense of pattern?

2 ★ In poem 12 how does the line length in the first four lines and the
     repetition of the "when" clauses support the meaning of those lines?
     Does the growing length underscore the speaker's growing irritation?

3 ★ In passage 13 how has Lawrence handled the verbs in the first four
     lines to help give a pattern to the poem? What other devices of repeti-
     tion has he used? What purpose is served by the repetition and promi-
     nent placement of "and"?

## Sound

### i

Sound, like rhythm, is a factor in everyday speech that the poet puts to maximum use. Sound, as a matter of fact, exerts a rather decisive influence upon rhythm in poetry, as you may have noticed when studying the questions in the preceding two sections. Frost, for instance, in his poem about the old dog (p. 79), makes us pronounce "old dog barks backward" with four heavy stresses, partly because the grammatical arrangement (the syntax) calls for four such speech stresses, as we have seen, and partly because the words begin and end with consonants that compel us to rearrange our lips and tongue as we move from one word to the next; the words cannot be hurried up or run together. Coleridge obtains the reverse effect with his illustration of the anapest—"With a leap and a bound the swift anapests throng." To see how far sound and syntax, operating together, control rhythm, try to give the same anapestic swing that you gave to Coleridge's line to this one, which has exactly the same number of syllables:

Rooms filled fast, watched pots fumed, cars parked wide, all hell heaved.

Like rhythm, sound is used in poetry to give pleasure for its own sake and to enhance or clarify meaning. Repetition of sound is often inherently enjoyable (although an excess of it may be highly annoying). The pleasure of repeating sounds is one reason (there are others, to be sure) for the appeal of limericks, where sounds repeat each other thick and fast:

> There once was a man from Nantucket
> Who kept all his cash in a bucket;
>     But his daughter, named Nan,
>     Ran away with a man,
> And as for the bucket, Nantucket.                             5
>
> But he followed the pair to Pawtucket—
> The man and the girl with the bucket;
>     And he said to the man
>     He was welcome to Nan,
> But as for the bucket, Pawtucket.                            10

ANONYMOUS

The pleasure of repeating sounds also has something to do with the enduring vogue of comic jingles:

> It isn't the cough
> That carries you off;
> It's the coffin
> They carry you off in.

ANONYMOUS

Pleasure in repetition also helps account for the persistence of all kinds of rhymes for counting out ("Eenie, meenie, meinie, mo"); for jogging the memory ("Thirty days hath September"); for circulating oddments of practical wisdom ("Early to bed, early to rise"); and for posing riddles:

> Little Nancy Etticoat
> With a white petticoat
> And a red nose;
> She has no feet or hands,
> The longer she stands                                    5
> The shorter she grows.

ANONYMOUS

Notice how the repetition in "Women" brightens the corner where we happen to be:

> I like lemon on my salmon,
> Some like salmon plain.
> It is much the same with women,
> By and large and in the main.
>
> If you want a chain reaction,                            5
> Leave your chain out in the rain.
> It is much the same with women,
> By and large and in the main.
>
> Once when I was just a human,
> Someone tampered with my brain.                          10
> It is much the same with women,
> By and large and in the main.

—Women<br>ANONYMOUS

But we notice again in these samples what we noticed before with rhythm—that simple repetition is not enough. To create pleasure rather than distaste there must be change as well. The dominant form of

recurrence-with-change in the sound of poetry is *rhyme,* as in "brain"
and "main" above, or "off" and "cough."

## ii

Other forms of recurrence-with-change, all closely related to rhyme, are
(1) *assonance,* a term which usually refers to the recurrence of vowel
sounds in the presence of changing consonant sounds, as in "chain" and
"same" in "Women"; (2) *consonance,* which usually refers to the recur-
rence of consonant sounds, especially final consonant sounds in the pres-
ence of differing vowel sounds, as in "bitch" and "botched" in "There Died
a Myriad" (p. 33); and (3) *alliteration,* which refers to recurrence of initial
sounds, especially initial consonant sounds, as in "like" and "lemon" or
"some" and "salmon" above. These names are of no particular importance,
but the effects they stand for *are* important, and will be found in all
poetry in obvious or subtle ways.

Consider the following excerpt from a poem that makes much of
sound effects.

[ 1 ]                              From *Lepanto*

GILBERT KEITH CHESTERTON (1874–1936)

Strong gongs groaning as the guns boom far,
Don John of Austria is going to the war;
Stiff flags straining in the night-blasts cold,
In the gloom black-purple, in the glint old-gold,
Torchlight crimson on the copper kettledrums,                           5
Then the tuckets,° then the trumpets, then the cannon, and he
    comes.
Don John laughing in the brave beard curled,
Spurning of his stirrups like the thrones of all the world,
Holding his head up for a flag of all the free.
Lovelight of Spain—hurrah!                                             10
Death-light of Africa!
Don John of Austria
Is riding to the sea.

---

°**tuckets:** fanfares.

QUESTIONS

1 ★ This is a passage from a poem on the battle of Lepanto, where, in
the sixteenth century, the Moslems were thrown back from the gates
of Christian Europe. The lines contain several instances of (a) as-
sonance, (b) consonance, and (c) alliteration. Point them out. Where
is rhyme found, apart from the ends of lines?

2 ★ Indicate seven instances in the first five lines where the sound and
syntax have forced a succession of three heavy stresses. Why is this
pattern so often repeated? What relation does it have to what the
passage is saying? What causes a change in the movement in line 6
and how does that change support what is said? How is the last word
of line 11 given an unusual pronunciation? Is this appropriate?

3 ★ In some poetry, sound is allowed to become so powerful that it dis-
tracts our attention from the sense—hypnotizes us, so to speak, and
then passes off shoddy goods on us. Do you detect any signs of this
problem in the foregoing passage? In line 4, for instance, could "gloom"
and "glint" change places without loss in sense? With improvement in
sense? Does "crimson" in line 5 seem to have been chosen for its sense?

Here is another excerpt, also from a poem much concerned with
sound:

[2]  From *General William Booth Enters into Heaven*
                VACHEL LINDSAY (1879–1931)

Booth led boldly with his big bass drum—
(Are you washed in the blood of the Lamb?)
The Saints smiled gravely and they said: "He's come."
(Are you washed in the blood of the Lamb?)
Walking lepers followed, rank on rank,                         5
Lurching bravos from the ditches dank,
Drabs from the alleyways and drug fiends pale—
Minds still passion-ridden, soul-powers frail:—
Vermin-eaten saints with moldly breath,
Unwashed legions with the ways of Death—                      10
(Are you washed in the blood of the Lamb?)

QUESTIONS

General William Booth, founder and longtime head of the Salvation Army, devoted his life to the service of the outcasts of society. The refrain "Are you washed in the blood of the Lamb?" is a familiar revivalist's cry, meaning roughly: Are you cleansed of sin by your belief in Christ?

1 ★ What is the metrical pattern of the stanza? The rhyme pattern?

2 ★ How has Lindsay used sound and syntax to accentuate the picture of General William Booth (pounding his "big bass drum") leading the triumphant parade of the "down and out" into Heaven?

3 ★ What would be lost if the refrain "Are you washed in the blood of the Lamb?" were eliminated?

Comment on the part played by assonance, consonance, alliteration, and rhyme in the following. What is the metrical pattern of each?

> When the hounds of spring are on winter's traces,
>     The mother of months in meadow or plain
> Fills the shadows and windy places
>     With lisp of leaves and ripple of rain;

> —From the "Chorus" of *Atalanta in Calydon*
>     ALGERNON CHARLES SWINBURNE (1837–1909)

> Till the slow sea rise and the sheer cliff crumble,
>     Till terrace and meadow the deep gulfs drink,
> Till the strength of the waves of the high tides humble
>     The fields that lessen, the rocks that shrink,
> Here now in his triumph where all things falter,      5
>     Stretched out on the spoils that his own hand spread,
> As a god self-slain on his own strange altar,
>     Death lies dead.

> —From *A Forsaken Garden*
>     ALGERNON CHARLES SWINBURNE (1837–1909)

> In Xanadu did Kubla Khan
>     A stately pleasure-dome decree:
> Where Alph, the sacred river, ran
>     Through caverns measureless to man
> Down to a sunless sea.      5

So twice five miles of fertile ground
With walls and towers were girdled round:

—From *Kubla Khan*

SAMUEL TAYLOR COLERIDGE (1772–1834)

In the following poem, sound is used with great subtlety. Examine it carefully:

[3]              *O Where Are You Going?*

W. H. AUDEN (1907–    )

"O where are you going?" said reader to rider,
"That valley is fatal when furnaces burn,
Yonder's the midden° whose odors will madden,
That gap is the grave where the tall return."

"O do you imagine," said fearer to farer,                    5
"That dusk will delay on your path to the pass,
Your diligent looking discover the lacking
Your footsteps feel from granite to grass?"

"O what was that bird," said horror to hearer,
"Did you see that shape in the twisted trees?          10
Behind you swiftly the figure comes softly,
The spot on your skin is a shocking disease?"

"Out of this house"—said rider to reader,
"Yours never will"—said farer to fearer,
"They're looking for you"—said hearer to horror,      15
As he left them there, as he left them there.

## QUESTIONS

1 ★ The poem abounds in assonance, consonance, and alliteration. Indicate several instances of each.

---

°**midden:** dunghill.

2 ⋆ What impulses of human behavior are referred to in the terms "reader," "fearer," and "horror"? What impulses are referred to in "rider," "farer," and "hearer"?

3 ⋆ If we think of "reader" and "rider," "fearer" and "farer," and "horror" and "hearer" as standing for opposite impulses, what is the advantage of the fact that the pairs sound *somewhat alike?*

4 ⋆ What questions are asked in each of the first three stanzas and what warnings (in a sense, answers) are given by the questioner? Notice, for instance, that lines 11 and 12 are in statement form but with a question intonation pattern (determined by the question mark). What answers are given in stanza four?

5 ⋆ In how many respects does stanza four differ from the rest? What reason might the poet have for making it different? Why isn't the last line of the poem:

> As they left them there, as they left them there.

or

> As he left him there, as he left him there.

## iii

Apart from giving pleasure, sound in poetry—like rhythm—may contribute powerfully to meaning, as we have already suggested in some of the questions to preceding poems. In some cases, and to a limited extent, the poet achieves this contribution to meaning by actual imitation. That is to say, a few words—called *onomatopoeic* words—have sounds that more or less imitate their meanings; examples are "snap," "crackle," and "buzz." Even when word sound does not imitate meaning, however, skillful placement of a word may be used to reinforce meaning or some aspect of it. In the lines by Tennyson quoted in an earlier section (p. 81), two words with sounds that partly imitate their meanings, "clanged" and "rang," are so placed among other sounds that all of them together tend to support the idea of armor echoing on rock ("clanged," "crag," "rang," "sharp-smitten," "dint"):

> . . . and all to left and right
> The bare black cliff clanged round him, as he based
> His foot on juts of slippery crag that rang
> Sharp-smitten with the dint of armèd heels.

The following stanza uses no words at all whose sounds imitate their meaning, yet rhythm and sound together are made to support the idea of a rooster's crowing:

> Then one he singles from the crew,
> And cheers the happy hen;
> With "How do you do," and "How do you do,"
> And "How do you do" again.

> —From *The Beggar's Opera*, II, iv
> JOHN GAY (1685–1732)

In English poetry there is almost no limit to the possible range of such effects. Here is John Milton supporting with an array of gutturals (hard sounds like *g* and *k*), labials (explosive sounds made with the lips, often used to express strong feelings of anger or revulsion), and nasals (sounds partly made in the nose, like *m* and *n*) the idea of primitive ferocity in a certain pagan god, *Moloch*. (The *Ammonites* were an Old Testament people. *Rabba* was their capital. *Argob* and *Basan* were districts in their territory, which lay between the rivers *Jabbok* and *Arnon*, east of the Jordan.)

> First, *Moloch*, horrid king, besmeared with blood
> Of human sacrifice, and parents' tears;
> Though, for the noise of drums and timbrels loud,
> Their children's cries unheard° that passed through fire
> To his grim idol. Him the Ammonite                    5
> Worshiped in Rabba and her watery plain,
> In Argob and in Basan, to the stream
> Of utmost Arnon.

> —From *Paradise Lost*, I
> JOHN MILTON (1608–1674)

Here is Alexander Pope supporting with round, empty, echoing *nd* and *um* sounds his description of a contemporary's poetry as mostly noise. Notice also the use of *internal rhyme* to help emphasize the sound pattern.

---

°**unheard:** were unheard.

Rend with tremendous sound your ears asunder,
With gun, drum, trumpet, blunderbuss, and thunder.

—From *The First Satire of the Second Book of Horace Imitated*
ALEXANDER POPE (1688–1744)

Here is Robert Browning supporting with quick explosive sounds the idea of a match being scratched:

A tap at the pane, the quick sharp scratch
And blue spurt of a lighted match,

—From *Meeting at Night*
ROBERT BROWNING (1812–1889)

and, with very different sounds, the idea of a small boat beaching in wet sand:

As I gain the cove with pushing prow,
And quench its speed i' the slushy sand.

—*Ibid.*

But the contribution of sound to meaning is by no means always so clear-cut as in these illustrations. Often all that we can say truthfully is that the sound in some obscure but important way does or does not harmonize with meaning. Consider this stanza, for example, which is sung as a dirge over a young girl believed to be dead:

Fear no more the heat o' the sun,
    Nor the furious winter's rages:
Thou thy worldly task hast done,
    Home art gone, and ta'en thy wages:
Golden lads and girls all must,                                    5
As chimney sweepers, come to dust.

—From *Cymbeline*, IV, ii
WILLIAM SHAKESPEARE (1564–1616)

Every experienced reader of poetry would agree that sound and sense in this poem are strikingly attuned to each other, but it is doubtful whether any one of them would describe the attunement in the same way, for it resists being put into words. Perhaps the very most we can suggest in such a case is that the sound is quiet, sweetly flowing, unobtrusive, and thus chimes with the poem's statement that death is a repose, and even possibly a fulfillment, to which all of us will come.

In the following poem, "Velvet Shoes," try to indicate as specifically as possible how sound seems to match sense. Perhaps we should say that sound *makes* sense in this poem. Literally, snow is cold and wet and not very much like "velvet." Is the snow cold or wet here? Is there any need for protection against it?

>Let us walk in the white snow
>  In a soundless space;
>With footsteps quiet and slow,
>  At a tranquil pace,
>  Under veils of white lace.                    5
>
>I shall go shod in silk
>  And you in wool,
>White as white cow's milk,
>  More beautiful
>  Than the breast of a gull.                    10
>
>We shall walk through the still town
>  In a windless peace;
>We shall step upon white down,
>  Upon silver fleece,
>  Upon softer than these.                       15
>
>We shall walk in velvet shoes:
>  Wherever we go
>Silence will fall like dews
>  On white silence below.
>  We shall walk in the snow.                    20

—*Velvet Shoes*
ELINOR WYLIE (1885–1928)

In a wholly different way sound also matches sense in the following poem. Each stanza says essentially the same thing. The title, "In Tenebris" means "In Darkness," the darkness of spiritual numbness and dead-

ness, summed up in the last word of the poem, "unhope." How does the
shortness of the lines, the distorted syntax (making the reading difficult),
and the word choice underscore the deadness the speaker feels?

[4]                            *In Tenebris (I)*
                         THOMAS HARDY (1840–1928)

Wintertime nighs;
But my bereavement pain
It cannot bring again:
    Twice no one dies.

Flower-petals flee;                                                        5
But since it once hath been,
No more that severing scene
    Can harrow me.

Birds faint in dread:
I shall not lose old strength                                             10
In the lone frost's black length:
    Strength long since fled!

Leaves freeze to dun;
But friends cannot turn cold
This season as of old                                                     15
    For him with none.

Tempests may scath;
But love cannot make smart
Again this year his heart
    Who no heart hath.                                                    20

Black is night's cope;
But death will not appall
One who, past doubtings all,
    Waits in unhope.

QUESTIONS

1 ⋆ The normal syntax of lines 2–3 would be "But it [wintertime] cannot bring again the pain of my bereavement." What is the normal syntax of lines 6–8 and 18–20? What is the effect of the distortions?

2 ⋆ What double meanings are there in "cope" (line 21) and "appall" (line 22)? What difference would there be if the last line were the more normal:

Waits with no hope.

# IV

## DEVICES
## OF COMPRESSION:
### The Poet's Shorthand

## Overstatement

### i

Since poetry is, among other things, a way of saying much in little, devices of compression and concentration, devices that help pack maximum meaning into minimum space, are essential to it.

Overstatement is one way of obtaining maximum emphasis, with economy. In overstatement, we emphasize what we mean by saying more than we literally mean, or at least more than is literally true. On this account, overstatement occurs with particular frequency and abandon in love poems, of all periods and at all levels of sophistication.

> You're the Nile,
> > You're the Tower of Pisa,
> You're the smile
> > Of the Mona Lisa . . .
> I'm a worthless check,                                             5
> > A total wreck,
> > > A flop,
> But if, baby, I'm the bottom, you're the top!

> —From *You're the Top*
> COLE PORTER (1895–1964)

A violet by a mossy stone
   Half hidden from the eye!
—Fair as a star, when only one
   Is shining in the sky.

—From *She Dwelt Among the Untrodden Ways*
WILLIAM WORDSWORTH (1770–1850)

Till a' the seas gang dry, my dear,
   And the rocks melt wi' the sun;
And I will luve thee still, my dear,
   While the sands o' life shall run.

—From *My Luve Is Like a Red, Red Rose*
ROBERT BURNS (1759–1796)

Alas, alas, who's injured by my love?
   What merchant's ships have my sighs drowned?
Who says my tears have overflowed his ground?

—From *The Canonization*
JOHN DONNE (1572–1631)

O, she doth teach the torches to burn bright!
It seems she hangs upon the cheek of night
Like a rich jewel in an Ethiop's ear.

—From *Romeo and Juliet,* I, v
WILLIAM SHAKESPEARE (1564–1616)

We must not suppose, however, that overstatement is used only by lovers or always for purposes of praise. It can serve any type of strong emotion. Here is a satiric instance from a famous political poem of eighteenth-century England:

The midwife laid her hand on his thick skull
With this prophetic blessing, "Be thou dull!"—

—From *Absalom and Achitophel,* II
JOHN DRYDEN (1631–1700)

Here is a tragic instance that we have seen before:

Out, out, brief candle!
Life's but a walking shadow, a poor player

That struts and frets his hour upon the stage
And then is heard no more:

—From *Macbeth*, V, v
WILLIAM SHAKESPEARE (1564–1616)

And here is a comic instance:

O, she misused me past the endurance of a block. An oak but with
one green leaf on it would have answered her. . . . She speaks poniards,°
and every word stabs. If her breath were as terrible as her terminations,°
she would infect to the North star.

—From *Much Ado About Nothing*, II, i
WILLIAM SHAKESPEARE (1564–1616)

## ii

Here are three poems illustrating some of the characteristic forms that
overstatement takes.

[1]                     *In Order To*

KENNETH PATCHEN (1911–1972)

Apply for the position (I've forgotten now for what) I had to
marry the Second Mayor's daughter by twelve noon. The order arrived
three minutes of.

I already had a wife; the Second Mayor was childless: but I did it.

Next they told me to shave off my father's beard. All right. No
matter that he'd been a eunuch, and had succumbed in early childhood:
I did it, I shaved him.

Then they told me to burn a village; next, a fair-sized town; then,
a city; a bigger city; a small, down-at-heels country; then one of "the
great powers"; then another (another, another)—In fact, they went
right on until they'd told me to burn up every man-made thing on the
face of the earth! And I did it, I burned away every last trace, I left
nothing, nothing of any kind whatever.

---

°**poniards:** daggers.    °**terminations:** her manner of speaking.

Then they told me to blow it all to hell and gone! And I blew it all to hell and gone (oh, didn't I!) . . .

Now, they said, put it back together again; put it all back the way it was when you started.

Well . . . it was my turn then to tell *them* something. Shucks, I didn't want any job that bad.

[2]                            *Constancy*

SIR JOHN SUCKLING (1609–1642)

Out upon it! I have loved
   Three whole days together;
And am like to love three more,
   If it prove fair weather.

Time shall molt away his wings,     5
   Ere he shall discover
In the whole wide world again
   Such a constant lover.

But the spite on 't is, no praise
   Is due at all to me;     10
Love with me had made no stays,
   Had it any been but she.

Had it any been but she,
   And that very face,
There had been at least ere this     15
   A dozen dozen in her place.

[3]                            *Sonnet 130*

WILLIAM SHAKESPEARE (1564–1616)

My mistress' eyes are nothing like the sun;
Coral is far more red than her lips' red;

If snow be white, why then her breasts are dun;
If hairs be wires, black wires grow on her head.
I have seen roses damasked,° red and white,     5
But no such roses see I in her cheeks,
And in some perfumes is there more delight
Than in the breath that from my mistress reeks.
I love to hear her speak, yet well I know
That music hath a far more pleasing sound.     10
I grant I never saw a goddess go;
My mistress, when she walks, treads on the ground:
   And yet, by heaven, I think my love as rare
   As any she belied with false compare.


## QUESTIONS

1 ★ What examples of overstatement do you find in each of the poems?

2 ★ Two of these poems get part of their effect by reversing or parodying a "normal" situation. State for poems 2 and 3 what the "normal" situation would be, and in what respects the poet has reversed or parodied it.

3 ★ According to one critic, poem 1 is about a fact of the human mind. "It is about the mind's ability to become so involved with *means* that it loses sight of *purpose;* so concerned with *processes* that it neglects *values.* If we want to understand how a whole nation could do or acquiesce in doing what the Germans did to the Jews under Hitler, this is the appalling fact about the mind from which we must begin." Assuming that this analysis of the poem is correct, with what "means" and "processes" does the speaker of the poem become involved? In what sense can he be said to have lost sight of purpose? Of value? Does he become conscious of these again in the end—or is he at the end blinder than ever? The story in the poem reminds us of folk tales and fairy tales—forms of literature associated with children and the childhood of a people. How does this fact help explain the poet's choice of this kind of story to carry his theme?

4 ★ In poem 2, lines 3–4 contain what looks like an implied slur by the lover on his lady. What is the slur? Stanza two contains a handsome

---

°damasked: pink.

compliment by the lover to himself. What is it? Stanza three turns
the compliment to himself into a compliment to the lady. How? In
stanza four the implied slur on the lady of stanza one is turned into
a further high compliment to her. How?

5 ★ How is the apparent slur turned into a compliment in poem 3?


### iii

Now consider these other poems that employ overstatement.


[4]                          *Sonnet 18*

WILLIAM SHAKESPEARE (1564–1616)

Shall I compare thee to a summer's day?
Thou art more lovely and more temperate.
Rough winds do shake the darling buds of May,
And summer's lease hath all too short a date.
Sometime too hot the eye of heaven shines,                            5
And often is his gold complexion dimmed.
And every fair from fair sometime declines,
By chance or nature's changing course untrimmed.°
But thy eternal summer shall not fade,
Nor lose possession of that fair thou owest,°                        10
Nor shall Death brag thou wander'st in his shade
When in eternal lines to time thou grow'st.
    So long as men can breathe, or eyes can see,
    So long lives this, and this gives life to thee.


## QUESTIONS

1 ★ What does the first line mean? In other words, is it a question or a
statement in the form of a question?

2 ★ In what ways is the person addressed compared with and made
superior to "a summer's day"? What shift in the comparison serves

---

°**untrimmed:** deprived of ornamentation.     °**owest:** own.

to make the exaggeration acceptable and not just fancifully compli-
mentary? In what sense will the lady's superiority never diminish?
Why is "lines" in line 12 the key word of the comparison? (What is
the "this" of line 14?)

3 ★ Put the last two lines into your own words.

4 ★ Which of the two sonnets, Sonnet 130 or Sonnet 18, seems most compli-
mentary and why? How do they differ as examples of overstatement
used to tell a truth?

[5]           *I Taste a Liquor Never Brewed*
                EMILY DICKINSON (1830–1886)

    I taste a liquor never brewed,
    From tankards scooped in pearl;
    Not all the vats upon the Rhine
    Yield such an alcohol!

    Inebriate of air am I,                                     5
    And debauchee of dew,
    Reeling, through endless summer days,
    From inns of molten blue.

    When landlords turn the drunken bee
    Out of the foxglove's door,                                10
    When butterflies renounce their drams,
    I shall but drink the more!

    Till seraphs swing their snowy hats,
    And saints to windows run,
    To see the little tippler                                  15
    Leaning against the sun!

## QUESTIONS

1 ★ What is the "liquor never brewed" that the speaker tastes? What does
"pearl" stand for in line 2? Explain as fully as possible each reference
that develops the drinking metaphor.

2 ⋆ What specifically is the exaggeration of stanza three? Could the events
suggested in lines 9–11 comes to pass? If they could not, what does the
speaker gain by saying that *when* they do, "I shall but drink the more"?

3 ⋆ How would you reply to someone who argued that the comparison is
inappropriate?

[6]                *As I Walked Out One Evening*
                   W. H. AUDEN (1907–    )

As I walked out one evening,
   Walking down Bristol Street,
The crowds upon the pavement
   Were fields of harvest wheat.

And down by the brimming river                                    5
   I heard a lover sing
Under an arch of the railway:
   "Love has no ending.

I'll love you, dear, I'll love you
   Till China and Africa meet,                          10
And the river jumps over the mountain
   And the salmon sing in the street.

I'll love you till the ocean
   Is folded and hung up to dry,
And the seven stars go squawking                                  15
   Like geese about the sky.

The years shall run like rabbits,
   For in my arms I hold
The Flower of the Ages,
   And the first love of the world."                     20

But all the clocks in the city
   Began to whirr and chime:

"O let not Time deceive you,
　　You cannot conquer Time.

In the burrows of the Nightmare                    25
　　Where Justice naked is,
Time watches from the shadow
　　And coughs when you would kiss.

In headaches and in worry
　　Vaguely life leaks away,                       30
And Time will have his fancy
　　Tomorrow or today.

Into many a green valley
　　Drifts the appalling snow;
Time breaks the threaded dances                    35
　　And the diver's brilliant bow.

O plunge your hands in water,
　　Plunge them in up to the wrist;
Stare, stare in the basin
　　And wonder what you've missed.                 40

The glacier knocks in the cupboard,
　　The desert sighs in the bed,
And the crack in the teacup opens
　　A lane to the land of the dead,

Where the beggars raffle the banknotes            45
　　And the Giant is enchanting to Jack,
And the Lily-white Boy is a Roarer,
　　And Jill goes down on her back.

O look, look in the mirror,
　　O look in your distress;                       50
Life remains a blessing
　　Although you cannot bless.

O stand, stand at the window
    As the tears scald and start;
You shall love your crooked neighbor                    55
    With your crooked heart."

It was late, late in the evening,
    The lovers they were gone;
The clocks had ceased their chiming,
    And the deep river ran on.                    60

## QUESTIONS

1 ★ Who is the main speaker in the poem? What speakers does he over-
hear?

2 ★ The mood of the speaker is implied in his instinctive comparison of
the crowds he sees to "harvest wheat." What is normally the fate of
"harvest wheat"? What is thus suggested about the crowds? How does
this comparison fit in with what the clocks seem to say to the speaker?

3 ★ Is the overstatement by the lover in stanzas three through five so
ludicrous as to be completely insincere, or is it meant to be flatteringly
amusing, or, perhaps, a combination of the two? The answer to the
question lies in an assessment of the clocks' reply to the lover. What is
the tone of the exaggerated reply—bantering, mocking, serious?

4 ★ What is true about human behavior that validates the statement "You
cannot conquer Time"? If the clocks (ironically, Time) use exagger-
ated statements to answer the lover's exaggeration, what is gained by
doing so? The answer is essentially good, sober advice: Why isn't it
given soberly? What is the advice? Do the "lovers" hear the advice?
Would they pay attention to it if they did? (Consider the implications
of the final stanza.)

⌊7⌋                    *The Scholars*

WILLIAM BUTLER YEATS (1865–1939)

Bald heads forgetful of their sins,
Old, learned, respectable bald heads

Edit and annotate the lines
That young men, tossing on their beds,
Rhymed out in love's despair                                  5
To flatter beauty's ignorant ear.

All shuffle there; all cough in ink;
All wear the carpet with their shoes;
All think what other people think;
All know the man their neighbor knows.                        10
Lord, what would they say
Did their Catullus° walk that way?

## QUESTIONS

1 ★ Why is the title of the poem "The Scholars"? Is the overstatement about the "young men" unflattering in the same sense that the overstatement about the "bald heads" is?

2 ★ What were "their sins" (line 1)? What are their sins now? Explain lines 7–10.

3 ★ The speaker thinks that the old men who annotate passionate poets' lines would exclaim if they saw "their Catullus" alive. Why does the speaker think so?

[ 8 ]                            *Incident*

COUNTEE CULLEN (1903–1946)

Once riding in old Baltimore,
    Heart-filled, head-filled with glee,
I saw a Baltimorean
    Keep looking straight at me.

Now I was eight and very small,                               5
    And he was no whit bigger,

---

°Catullus: a Roman poet who celebrated, in terms we would consider bluntly realistic, the life and loves of a young man about town. The realism has often disappeared in "translation."

And so I smiled, but he poked out
His tongue and called me "Nigger."

I saw the whole of Baltimore
From May until December:                        10
Of all the things that happened there
That's all that I remember.


## QUESTIONS

1 * What *is* the "incident" that the poem describes? What are we told
in lines 2, 5–6 that accounts for what the speaker did? What are we
told in lines 1, 3–4, that accounts for what the "Baltimorean" did?
What added effect is obtained here by calling Baltimore "old Balti-
more"? by calling an eight-year-old a "Baltimorean"? by saying that
he "poked" out his tongue rather than (saying) "stuck" it out?

2 * Does the last stanza contain an overstatement? If so, what literal truth
is it used to convey? If not, explain how it can be a literal truth as it
stands.

3 * What do the formal characteristics of the poem—its regularities of
rhyme and rhythm, its division into equal stanzas, its quiet language—
contribute to its total effect? (Note that the speaker does not apply
any shrill language to the other boy or to the event, even in retro-
spect: the boy remains a "Baltimorean" and the event simply an
"Incident.")


## Understatement

Understatement is of course precisely the opposite of overstatement. In
understatement we emphasize what we mean by saying less than we
literally mean, or less than is literally true. For an effective example, we
may look back for a moment at Robert Frost's "Out, Out—" (p. 62). The
speech in *Macbeth* (p. 63) to which, as we saw, Frost's title alludes takes
the expression of futility and despair about as far as overstatement will
go. Macbeth speaks as if the analogy, which does indeed exist, between
a human life and an actor's "hour" upon the stage were the literal truth

about the lives of men and women. Frost's speaker in "Out, Out—" moves in the reverse direction. He also communicates a sense of futility and despair, but by understatement. In his description of the boy's death, no word that does justice to the literal situation is allowed to appear. No one—so far as we are told—gasps, swallows hard, swears, prays, or is even slightly shaken. Instead,

> Little—less—nothing! and that ended it.
> No more to build on there. And they, since they
> Were not the one dead, turned to their affairs.

Hardy obtains a somewhat analogous effect, though slighter, with the description of war that he puts in his speaker's mouth in the last stanza of "The Man He Killed" (p. 31): "Yes; quaint and curious war is! . . ." This again is a good deal less than the situation justifies, since it comes from a man who, obviously of a sympathetic and kindly nature, has been forced by war to kill a fellow human being. But what Hardy's speaker leaves out we tend to fill in with our own imaginations, and this is one reason for the great effectiveness of understatement in obtaining emphasis. Consider whether or not understatement is effective in the following two examples:

[1]                              *Portrait*

E. E. CUMMINGS (1894–1962)

Buffalo Bill's
defunct
        who used to
        ride a watersmooth-silver

                                stallion                              5
and   break   onetwothreefourfive   pigeonsjustlikethat
                                                Jesus

he was a handsome man
                        and what i want to know is
how do you like your blueeyed boy                    10
Mister Death

[2]                          *Losses*

RANDELL JARRELL (1914–1965)

It was not dying: everybody died.
It was not dying: we had died before
In the routine crashes—and our fields°
Called up the papers, wrote home to our folks,
And the rates° rose, all because of us.                     5
We died on the wrong page of the almanac,
Scattered on mountains fifty miles away;
Diving on haystacks, fighting with a friend,
We blazed up on the lines° we never saw.
We died like ants or pets or foreigners.                    10
(When we left high school nothing else had died
For us to figure we had died like.)

In our new planes, with our new crews, we bombed
The ranges by the desert or the shore,
Fired at towed targets, waited for our scores—              15
And turned into replacements and woke up
One morning, over England, operational.
It wasn't different: but if we died
It was not an accident but a mistake
(But an easy one for anyone to make).                       20
We read our mail and counted up our missions—
In bombers named for girls, we burned
The cities we had learned about in school—
Till our lives wore out; our bodies lay among
The people we had killed and never seen.                    25
When we lasted long enough they gave us medals;
When we died they said, "Our casualties were low."
They said, "Here are the maps"; we burned the cities.

It was not dying—no, not ever dying;

---

°**fields:** airfields    °**rates:** insurance rates    °**lines:** powerlines.

But the night I died I dreamed that I was dead,                    30
And the cities said to me: "Why are you dying?
We are satisfied, if you are; but why did I die?"


## QUESTIONS

1 ★ What examples of understatement are there in any of the poems used
to illustrate overstatement? Consider particularly poems 1, 2, and 3.

2 ★ "Portrait" treats a serious subject—the death of a well-known figure—
in a lighthearted manner. The "i" of the poem is no boy, but he uses
the idiom of boyish wonder to suggest that even though Buffalo Bill
is dead, he remains just as vital as ever: he is a "blueeyed boy" who
has moved in with old "Mister Death," who certainly ought to ap-
preciate what he got. Show how the understatement, the almost irrever-
ent attitude toward death, actually gives the fact of death more proper
reverence than a somber treatment would give. Consider the details of
the "portrait" of Buffalo Bill in action, the use of such words as "de-
funct" instead of "dead," and the way the lines are printed on the
page.

3 ★ "Losses" is another poem about death. As the title suggests, this poem,
too, treats death rather casually: "losses" are things that get added up
for use in keeping statistics. What lines clearly establish the pattern
of understatement?

4 ★ In "Losses" who is the speaker? What specifically does he recall in
the first fifteen lines? In what tone are these experiences recalled? How
does line 10 underscore the attitude adopted, and how is it reinforced
in lines 11–12? What do lines 16–28 deal with and how have the first
twelve lines prepared for the treatment of these experiences?

5 ★ Line 29 repeats the opening words. What deepened meaning have the
intervening lines given to them? What is ironic about line 30? How do
the last two lines employ both overstatement and understatement?

6 ★ How is understatement used in "My Papa's Waltz" (p. 69)? Consider
the use of "romped," "unfrown," "beat time on my head," "waltzed me
off to bed," and the almost jingly regularity of the rhythm. How does
the speaker communicate the coarse exuberance of the father and the
breath-holding fear of the boy? In what sense was the father's drunken
dance a "waltz" (to whom?) and in what sense was it not?

## Irony and paradox

### i

In overstatement we intensify meaning by saying more than we literally mean or than is literally true. In understatement we intensify meaning by saying less than we literally mean or than is literally true. With *irony* and *paradox* we intensify meaning by saying something different from what we literally mean or from what is literally true. A *paradox* is a compressed way of making a single truth grow from two elements that literally contradict each other: it is a spark that leaps between a negatively and positively charged pole. "Damn with faint praise" (Alexander Pope), "The last shall be first" (New Testament), "The wise through excess of wisdom is made a fool" (Ralph Waldo Emerson), "Poetry is a language that tells us something that cannot be said" (Edwin Arlington Robinson)—all these are paradoxes in that two seemingly contradictory elements generate between them a meaning that cannot be got at so economically in any other way. To explain the idea underlying "Damn with faint praise," for instance, we not only have to use a great many more words than Pope used, but we lose the impact, the shock value, which paradox ordinarily has for us.

Paradox does not absolutely require that its contradictory elements be brought out by contradictory words, as they are in the foregoing examples. We can still detect the contradiction in the idea of a person's being at the end of a line yet somehow getting through a gate sooner than those preceding him ("The last shall be first"), no matter how it is phrased. Yet there is no doubt that paradox strengthens and moves toward its perfection when the contradictory elements in the situation are underscored by contradictory words; and you will find it difficult if not impossible in some cases—for example, in the case of the paradox quoted from Emerson —to describe the contradictory situation adequately apart from some form of verbal contradiction.

With *irony* this dependence on wording is not the case. There is a *verbal* irony, very common in our daily speech, which we use when we exclaim "You're a big help!" to someone who has awkwardly knocked all our books out of our hands while he was stooping to pick up our hat; and this kind of irony is found in poetry frequently enough. But the commonest and most powerful form that irony can take, in poetry and literature generally, is that of *situation*, and for this irony no particular wording is required. A man labors all his life, denying himself every pleasure, to lay up a fortune for his children to inherit, and then sees them all die before his own death. A Macbeth murders to get what he thinks he covets only to find it has turned to ashes in his hands. An Oedipus sets out to find the source of the evil that has infected his kingdom and discovers that it is himself. A Proud Maisie walks abroad on a spring morning glowing with thoughts of love and marriage, but actually her bridegroom will be death and her bridal bed the grave. Such ironies as these are ironies of situation.

Related both to irony of situation and to verbal irony is a third form of irony that we usually call *dramatic*. This appears whenever a speaker in a literary work says something with an application or a depth of meaning that we or others see but he does not. Thus King Duncan, commenting in *Macbeth* on the treason of one of his most trusted subjects, says, "There's no art to find the mind's construction in the face," just as Macbeth, who is going to prove a traitor very soon, enters the room. Duncan's comment has an application that he does not see. Similarly, after the assassination of Julius Caesar in Shakespeare's play of that name, Brutus says to his fellow assassins:

> . . . let us bathe our hands in Caesar's blood
> Up to the elbows, and besmear our swords;
> Then walk we forth, even to the market place,
> And waving our red weapons o'er our heads,
> Let's all cry, "Peace, freedom, and liberty!"          5

> —From *Julius Caesar*, III, i
> WILLIAM SHAKESPEARE (1564–1616)

In the speech of Brutus, there are two layers of dramatic irony. The first lies in the ironical contrast (of which Brutus is wholly unaware) between the bloody assassins and the cry "Peace, freedom, and liberty!" The second lies in the ironical contrast between the "peace, freedom, and liberty" which they wanted to bring Rome and the discord and carnage which, as the rest of the play shows, they actually did bring. The irony of the word "waiting" in the young lady's speech in "Piazza Piece" (p. 36) is also of this dramatic kind when she utters it for the second time: "I am a lady young in beauty waiting." She is waiting, all right. But she has not stopped to think (as we have been made to do) for whom it is that she is waiting.

The two poems which follow, "Sir Patrick Spence" and "Ozymandias," are filled with irony of all sorts. The questions on page 134 will help you identify it.

[1]                          *Sir Patrick Spence*

ANONYMOUS

The king sits in Dumferling toune,°
   Drinking the blude-reid° wine:
"O whar will I get guid° sailor,
   To sail this schip of mine?"

Up and spak an eldern knicht,°                                    5
   Sat at the kings richt° kne:
"Sir Patrick Spence is the best sailor,
   That sails upon the se."

The king has written a braid° letter,
   And signd it wi his hand,                              10
And sent it to Sir Patrick Spence,
   Was walking on the sand.

The first line that Sir Patrick red,
   A loud lauch° lauchèd he;
The next line that Sir Patrick red,                              15
   The teir blinded his ee.

"O wha is this has don this deid,
   This ill deid don to me,
To send me out this time o' the yeir,
   To sail upon the se!                                    20

"Mak hast, mak hast, my mirry men all,
   Our guid schip sails the morne":
"O say na sae,° my master deir,
   For I fear a deadlie storme.

"Late, late yestreen° I saw the new moone,                       25
   Wi the auld moone in hir arme,

---

°**toune:** town.     °**blude-reid:** blood-red.     °**guid:** good.     °**knicht:** knight.
°**richt:** right.     °**braid:** broad (official).     °**lauch:** laugh.     °**na sae:** not so.
°**yestreen:** yesterday evening.

And I feir, I feir, my deir master,
    That we will cum to harme."

O our Scot nobles wer richt laith°
    To weet° their cork-heild schoone;°         30
But lang owre a'° the play wer playd,
    Thair hats they swam aboone.

O lang, lang may their ladies sit,
    Wi thair fans into thair hand,
Or eir they se Sir Patrick Spence         35
    Cum sailing to the land.

O lang, lang may the ladies stand,
    Wi thair gold kems in thair hair,
Waiting for thair ain deir lords,
    For they'll se thame na mair.         40

Haf owre,° haf owre to Aberdour,
    It's fiftie fadom° deip,
And thair lies guid Sir Patrick Spence,
    Wi the Scots lords at his feit.

[2]                     *Ozymandias*

PERCY BYSSHE SHELLEY (1792–1822)

I met a traveler from an antique land
Who said: Two vast and trunkless legs of stone
Stand in the desert . . . Near them, on the sand,
Half sunk, a shattered visage lies, whose frown,
And wrinkled lip, and sneer of cold command,         5
Tell that its sculptor well those passions read
Which yet survive, stamped on these lifeless things,
The hand that mocked them, and the heart that fed:

---

°**laith:** loath (reluctant).   °**weet:** wet.   °**cork-heild schoone:** cork-heeled shoes.   °**owre a':** before all.   °**owre:** over.   °**fadom:** fathom.

And on the pedestal these words appear:
"My name is Ozymandias, king of kings:                                    10
Look on my works, ye Mighty, and despair!"
Nothing beside remains. Round the decay
Of that colossal wreck, boundless and bare
The lone and level sands stretch far away.


QUESTIONS

1 ★ In poem 1, what apparently does the King order in his letter (stanza
    three)? Why does Sir Patrick first laugh on reading the order? Why
    later does the tear spring to his eye? What feeling do the Scots nobles
    have about making the trip? Why are their feelings so different from
    Sir Patrick's? What is the attitude of the Scots ladies as they wait in
    lines 33–34? What shows their attitude has changed in lines 37–38?

2 ★ Point out two examples of irony of situation in poem 1. There is dra-
    matic irony in the words "guid" and "best" in lines 3 and 7. Explain.
    There is verbal irony in lines 33–36. Explain.

3 ★ In poem 2, whose passions "yet survive . . . the hand that mocked
    them and the heart that fed?" (lines 7–8). Whose "heart" fed them?
    Whose "hand" mocked them? How?

4 ★ What instruction does Ozymandias give to those who pass by the
    pedestal of his statue? Whom did he expect to read these instructions?
    Who actually does read them? Where are the "works" the instructions
    speak of? Whose work actually *has* survived? Is it true that the arts
    of a nation survive most of its other manifestations? What do we have
    left from ancient Egypt? Ancient Greece? Ancient China? What is
    most likely to remain from our age in A.D. 4000?

5 ★ Poem 2 contains verbal irony, dramatic irony, and irony of situation.
    State where and explain.


## ii

Though irony and paradox spring up everywhere in poetry (and in other
forms of literature as well), the following poems contain some particularly
notable examples:

[3]                    *The Wood-Pile*

ROBERT FROST (1874–1963)

Out walking in the frozen swamp one gray day,
I paused and said, "I will turn back from here.
No, I will go on farther—and we shall see."
The hard snow held me, save where now and then
One foot went through. The view was all in lines          5
Straight up and down of tall slim trees
Too much alike to mark or name a place by
So as to say for certain I was here
Or somewhere else: I was just far from home.
A small bird flew before me. He was careful               10
To put a tree between us when he lighted,
And say no word to tell me who he was
Who was so foolish as to think what *he* thought.
He thought that I was after him for a feather—
The white one in his tail; like one who takes             15
Everything said as personal to himself.
One flight out sideways would have undeceived him.
And then there was a pile of wood for which
I forgot him and let his little fear
Carry him off the way I might have gone,                  20
Without so much as wishing him goodnight.
He went behind it to make his last stand.
It was a cord of maple, cut and split
And piled—and measured, four by four by eight.
And not another like it could I see.                      25
No runner tracks in this year's snow looped near it.
And it was older sure than this year's cutting,
Or even last year's or the year's before.
The wood was gray and the bark warping off it
And the pile somewhat sunken. Clematis                    30
Had wound strings round and round it like a bundle.
What held it though on one side was a tree

Still growing, and on one a stake and prop,
These latter about to fall. I thought that only
Someone who lived in turning to fresh tasks                    35
Could so forget his handiwork on which
He spent himself, the labor of his ax,
And leave it there far from a useful fireplace
To warm the frozen swamp as best it could
With the slow smokeless burning of decay.                      40


## QUESTIONS

1 ★ Put into your own words the basic irony of the situation involving the
woodpile. Why was the wood cut in the first place? What will eventu-
ally happen to it? How does it make sense to say that it can "warm
the frozen swamp" with the "smokeless burning of decay"?

2 ★ What other examples of irony are there in the poem? What purpose is
served by the speaker's encounter with the suspicious bird?


[4]                    *To an Athlete Dying Young*
                    A. E. HOUSMAN (1859–1936)

The time you won your town the race
We chaired you through the market place;
Man and boy stood cheering by,
And home we brought you shoulder-high.

Today, the road all runners come,                              5
Shoulder-high we bring you home,
And set you at your threshold down,
Townsman of a stiller town.

Smart lad, to slip betimes away
From fields where glory does not stay                          10
And early though the laurel grows
It withers quicker than the rose.

Eyes the shady night has shut
Cannot see the record cut,
And silence sounds no worse than cheers          15
After earth has stopped the ears:

Now you will not swell the rout
Of lads that wore their honors out,
Runners whom renown outran
And the name died before the man.                20

So set, before its echoes fade,
The fleet foot on the sill of shade,
And hold to the low lintel up
The still-defended challenge-cup.

And round that early-laureled head              25
Will flock to gaze the strengthless dead,
And find unwithered on its curls
The garland briefer than a girl's.

## QUESTIONS

1 ★ What ironic situation is carefully developed in the first two stanzas?
How has the speaker closely paralleled the two occurrences that would
seem on the surface to be so removed from each other?

2 ★ How has he prepared for the irony of referring to the dead runner as
a "smart lad"? What does the "laurel" stand for? The "rose"? Ironically,
under what conditions can each remain unwithered?

[5]                    *Holy Sonnet 10*
                  JOHN DONNE (1572–1631)

Death, be not proud, though some have called thee
Mighty and dreadful, for thou art not so;
For those whom thou think'st thou dost overthrow

Die not, poor Death, nor yet canst thou kill me.
From rest and sleep, which but thy pictures be,                    5
Much pleasure, then from thee much more must flow;
And soonest our best men with thee do go,
Rest of their bones and soul's delivery.
Thou'rt slave to fate, chance, kings, and desperate men,
And dost with poison, war, and sickness dwell;                    10
And poppy or charms can make us sleep as well,
And better than thy stroke. Why swell'st thou then?
One short sleep past, we wake eternally,
And death shall be no more. Death, thou shalt die.


QUESTIONS

1 ★ What is the paradox stated in the last line of "Holy Sonnet 10"? How
    has it been prepared for? In other words, how is the argument de-
    veloped that leads up to it? (Line 13 asserts the speaker's belief in an
    afterlife.) What earlier paradoxes are there?

2 ★ What is the basic metrical pattern? In what lines is it most clearly re-
    vealed? What obvious variations are there, and what is their effective-
    ness in the poem?

3 ★ What is the tone of the poem? Arrogant? Flippant? Smug? Mocking?
    Nonchalant? Calm? None of these?


[6]                         *What Are Years?*

                    MARIANNE MOORE (1887–1972)

        What is our innocence,
    what is our guilt? All are
        naked, none is safe. And whence
    is courage: the unanswered question,
    the resolute doubt,—                                          5
        dumbly calling, deafly listening—that
    in misfortune, even death,
        encourages others
        and in its defeat, stirs

the soul to be strong? He                              10
sees deep and is glad, who
        accedes to mortality
and in his imprisonment, rises
upon himself as
the sea in a chasm, struggling to be                   15
free and unable to be,
        in its surrendering
        finds its continuing.

So he who strongly feels,
behaves. The very bird,                                20
        grown taller as he sings, steels
his form straight up. Though he is captive,
his mighty singing
says, satisfaction is a lowly
thing, how pure a thing is joy.                        25
        This is mortality,
        this is eternity.

## QUESTIONS

1 ★ What questions are raised in the first two lines? What is the answer
    given in lines 2–3? The question in lines 3–4 is oddly put: "And
    whence is courage?" Why is it not the more normal "What is cour-
    age?" or "Whence comes courage?" What connection does the question
    have with the first two questions? Lines 4–10 identify courage in a
    series of paradoxes. Explain them.

2 ★ Stanzas two and three are built around two extended comparisons.
    In what terms is courage described in stanza two? What does the
    sea in a chasm do? What is the paradox in lines 17–18 and how has
    it been resolved?

3 ★ What is the comparison in stanza three? Where is the bird? Why is
    "steels" a particularly appropriate verb in the development of the
    comparison? What is the difference between "satisfaction" and "joy"?

4 ★ What does "this" refer to in lines 26–27? The dictionary meanings of
    "mortality" ("subject to death") and "eternity" ("not subject to

death") would seem to deny that both words can be applied to the same condition. Paradoxically, how can they be, as demonstrated in the poem?

5 ★ What is the answer to the title?

[7]                    *Richard Cory*

EDWIN ARLINGTON ROBINSON (1869–1935)

Whenever Richard Cory went down town,
We people on the pavement looked at him:
He was a gentleman from sole to crown,
Clean favored, and imperially slim.

And he was always quietly arrayed,                    5
And he was always human when he talked;
But still he fluttered pulses when he said,
"Good-morning," and he glittered when he walked.

And he was rich—yes, richer than a king—
And admirably schooled in every grace:                    10
In fine, we thought that he was everything
To make us wish that we were in his place.

So on we worked, and waited for the light,
And went without the meat, and cursed the bread;
And Richard Cory, one calm summer night,                    15
Went home and put a bullet through his head.

QUESTIONS

1 ★ On what does the irony of "Richard Cory" seem to depend? Simply on the trick ending? Or is it a trick ending? Is the outcome prepared for in any way? If, in a sense, it is not prepared for, how does that fact reinforce the underlying irony of the poem?

2 ★ How carefully has the speaker seen his man? In what terms does he describe him? Why does he say "from sole to crown" (line 3) instead of "from head to foot" (ignoring the problem of rhyme for the mo-

ment)? What kind of people think other people "glitter" when they walk, and use phrases like "clean favored" and "quietly arrayed"? What is the speaker trying to suggest about Richard Cory? More important, what does he reveal about his own powers of discrimination? (Remember, he is the same person who uses such language as "went without the meat, and cursed the bread.") How much do people like the speaker understand of those they really do not know? What have these considerations got to do with the problem raised in question 1? What double irony is there in the poem?

[ 8 ]                              *The Negro*

JAMES A. EMANUEL (1921–      )

Never saw him.
Never can.
Hypothetical,
Haunting man:

Eyes a-saucer,                                                    5
Yessir, boss-sir,
Dice a-clicking,
Razor flicking.

The-ness froze him
In a dance.                                                       10
A-ness never
Had a chance.

QUESTIONS

1 * The point of the poem is obvious: what society has created is a stereotype of "the Negro" that prevents its seeing Black people as individual human beings. In the light of this overall point, explain in detail what the poet means by (a) "Never saw him" (b) "Never can" (c) "Hypothetical" (d) "Haunting" (e) "The-ness froze him." What is the relation of the "hypothetical" man of lines 3–4 to the attributes described in lines 5–8? How do they exemplify "The-ness"? and preclude "A-ness"?

2 * Why is the title of the poem appropriate?

[ 9 ]                       *London*
                WILLIAM BLAKE (1757–1827)

I wander through each chartered street,
Near where the chartered Thames does flow,
And mark in every face I meet
Marks of weakness, marks of woe.

In every cry of every man,                                      5
In every infant's cry of fear,
In every voice, in every ban,
The mind-forged manacles I hear:

How the chimney sweeper's cry
Every blackening church appalls,                               10
And the hapless soldier's sigh
Runs in blood down palace walls.

But most, through midnight streets I hear
How the youthful harlot's curse
Blasts the newborn infant's tear,                             15
And blights with plagues the marriage hearse.


QUESTIONS

1 ★ Discuss the pattern of ironies that make up Blake's indictment of man's
    inhumanity to man in "London." How can the "manacles" of line 8
    be "mind-forged"? How and why does the "chimney sweeper's cry"
    appall "every blackening church"? What is "blackening" the church?
    What should the church do about the use of young children as chim-
    ney sweepers? What double meaning is there in "appalls"?

2 ★ In what sense can a soldier's sigh run "in blood down palace walls"?
    What have palaces to do with soldiers? What does "sigh" mean here?

3 ★ Why does the fourth stanza start with "But most"? What is the "youth-
    ful [why "youthful"?] harlot's curse"? How can her curse blast "the
    newborn infant's tear"? How can it blight with "plagues"? Why does
    the speaker conjoin the words "marriage" and "hearse"?

## Comparison

### i

The most important of all devices for saying much in little in poetry is comparison. Our ordinary speech is full of comparisons, and most of us are able to recognize, when we stop to think, those which are conveyed by means of *simile* or *metaphor*. "It seems she hangs upon the cheek of night,/Like a rich jewel in an Ethiop's ear." Romeo says that Juliet is hanging like some adornment on the cheek of night, and then, with the use of "like" to introduce the specific comparison, he likens her to a "jewel" hanging from "an Ethiop's ear." If he had said, "She is a jewel hanging from an Ethiop's ear," we would have what is technically referred to as a *metaphor*. If "like" or "as" is used to make the comparison ("like a rich jewel . . ."), we have a *simile*. Often the word *metaphor* is used in a broader sense to refer to any comparison in which one thing is described in terms of another. In questions on the poems that follow we will usually use the term *metaphor* in this broader sense.

We can see the process of metaphor at work in many of the poems we have looked at already. For a few examples consider: "Like a small gray coffeepot" ("The Gray Squirrel," p. 5); "whereon a dozen staunch and leal/citizens did *graze at*" ("A Man Who Had Fallen Among Thieves," p. 15; notice that here grammar is being used metaphorically, for not only is there the comparison with sheep in "graze," but there is also the grammatical comparison with "gaze at"); "For an old *bitch* gone in the teeth" ("There Died a Myriad," p. 33); "I am a gentleman in a *dust-coat*" ("Piazza Piece," p. 36); "the blond *assassin*" ("Apparently with No Surprise," p. 61); "*Golden* lads and girls all must,/As *chimney sweepers*, come to *dust*" (Fear No More the Heat o' the Sun," p. 111). You can find other examples in the previous poem, "London," and in the following:

[1]                     *Digging for China*
                  RICHARD WILBUR (1921–    )

"Far enough down is China," somebody said.
"Dig deep enough and you might see the sky
As clear as at the bottom of a well.
Except it would be real—a different sky.
Then you could burrow down until you came        5
To China! Oh, it's nothing like New Jersey.

There's people, trees, and houses, and all that
But much, much different. Nothing looks the same."

I went and got the trowel out of the shed
And sweated like a coolie all that morning.                        10
Digging a hole beside the lilac bush,
Down on my hands and knees. It was a sort
Of praying, I suspect. I watched my hand
Dig deeper and darker, and I tried and tried
To dream a place where nothing was the same.                        15
The trowel never did break through to blue.

Before the dream could weary of itself
My eyes were tired of looking into darkness,
My sunbaked head of hanging down a hole.
I stood up in a place I had forgotten,                              20
Blinking and staggering while the earth went round
And showed me silver barns, the fields dozing
In palls of brightness, patens growing and gone
In the tides of leaves, and the whole sky china blue.
Until I got my balance back again                                   25
All that I saw was China, China, China.

## QUESTIONS

1 ★ Who is the speaker? What kind of person is he? What kind of person
is the "somebody" of the first stanza?

2 ★ Explain as fully as possible the metaphors in lines 22–24. Why are the
barns "silver"? What suggestions are there in "palls of brightness" (be
sure you know what "palls" are)? What are "patens" and why would
the speaker in his condition see them "growing and gone/In the tides
of leaves"? What is ironic and appropriate about "china blue"?

3 ★ What is the speaker looking for? What does he think it will be like?
Ironically, how does he find it? Is it what he thought (or hoped) it
would be like? What irony is there in the word "balance" (line 25)?
What does physical "balance" do to his spiritual equilibrium?

4 * How is the poem a metaphor for one kind of human behavior? How do you know that it is spiritual equilibrium the speaker is talking about? (Note lines 12–13.)

[ 2 ]                          *Harlem*

LANGSTON HUGHES (1902–1967)

What happens to a dream deferred?

Does it dry up
like a raisin in the sun?
Or fester like a sore—
And then run?
Does it stink like rotten meat?                                    5
Or crust and sugar over—
like a syrupy sweet?

Maybe it just sags
like a heavy load.

*Or does it explode?*                                             10

QUESTIONS

1 * How would you define the "dream" that Hughes refers to? Why is it "deferred"? Compare and contrast with this dream the one spoken of in Wilbur's poem.

2 * The poem tentatively suggests six possible effects that deferment may have on a dream. What does the poet gain from choosing here to be so tentative—from asking rather than telling us?

3 * Each of the first five effects is elaborated by a simile that makes the effect claimed seem natural and inevitable—e.g. drying up "like a raisin in the sun," festering "like a sore," and so on. Show how this procedure makes the sixth effect stand out like the very explosion it describes.

## ii

With other forms of comparison we may be less familiar than we are with simile and metaphor, because we have not stopped to realize, as we used them, what they were. *Allusion* is one of these. Allusion brings objects or ideas together for comparison in precisely the same way that metaphor and simile do. In the midst of Romeo's combined metaphor and simile about Juliet, for instance, there is also an allusion—to the Ethiop. Juliet's youthful beauty lights up the night the way a bright jewel lights up the cheek of an Ethiopian prince. The reader has to recognize the allusion to the Ethiopian prince before the comparison can have full effect. Explanations of allusions that refer to people, to places, to historical events, or to works of literature can usually be found in different kinds of reference books. But often they call up a tradition, and then the necessary information can only be had from experience. "Proud Maisie" (p. 34) and "La Belle Dame sans Merci" (p. 49), for instance, *allude* to the tradition of the folk ballad. Auden's "As I Walked Out One Evening" (p. 122) alludes jokingly to the tradition of love poetry in which fantastic claims are made about the longevity of the lover's faithfulness. Shakespeare's "Sonnet 130" (p. 118) alludes to the tradition of the "blazon of beauty," which is a lover's description of the several beauties of his loved one from the crown of her pretty head right down to her charming toes. Kenneth Patchen's "In Order To" (p. 117) alludes to the type of folk tale in which the hero has to perform all sorts of impossible feats in order to win the king's daughter. For these matters there is no dictionary and can be none. As we have to learn about baseball by watching it, we have to learn about literature by reading it.

## iii

Two further forms of comparison to be considered here are *juxtaposition* and *pun*. *Juxtaposition* is a comparison achieved by simply placing the names of objects side by side—in other words, juxtaposing them, in such a way as to imply that the listener or reader should look for a connection. When Pope, for example, writes of midday in "The Rape of the Lock" (I, 15–16) and says:

> Now lap dogs give themselves the rousing shake,
> And sleepless lovers, just at twelve, awake:

we can look beyond the comic paradox of the "sleepless lovers" who awake at noon to see that the juxtaposition of "lap dogs" and "lovers" is an implied comparison, for the context has already made it clear that in the world this poem describes—the world of fashionable gentlemen-about-town, who have nothing to do but pay compliments to pretty debu-tantes—lovers and lap dogs can hardly be distinguished from each other. Ransom, similarly, in "Piazza Piece" (p. 36) implies a comparison by juxtaposing the lady's beauty, the roses on her trellis, and the moon—three things that fade. Gray, at the close of the first stanza of "Elegy Written in a Country Churchyard" (p. 95), manages to imply a connection between the falling darkness and the melancholy quiet of the speaker by juxtaposing "darkness" and "me." The great virtue of juxtaposition, as these instances show, is that it is unobtrusive. One may make a witty com-parison this way (lap dogs and lovers) without calling attention to one's wittiness, or a sober comparison (darkness and me) without falling into the self-consciousness of "The darkness of the evening is my darkness."

*Puns* are familiar enough to all of us, but not everyone knows how wide their range is or to what heights of meaning they may rise. At the bottom of their range, we have of course the "execrable pun," the kind which has given the whole species a bad odor: "Why did the moron throw himself from the Hotel Astor? Because he wanted to make a hit on Broad-way." At the top of its range, on the other hand, we have on one side the genuinely witty pun, as in this example, "A Happy Time":

> There was a young fellow named Hall,
> Who fell in the spring in the fall;
> 'Twould have been a sad thing
> If he'd died in the spring,
> But he didn't—he died in the fall.          5

> —*A Happy Time*
> ANONYMOUS

and on the other side, still at the top, the deeply serious pun, which often compresses into a single word the struggle of two passions, two ideas, two ideals, or even two different worlds. In Shakespeare's *Hamlet,* the young prince, shocked by the corruption he has found in his mother and the knowledge that his father was murdered by his uncle, comes upon Ophelia, the girl he loves, praying. Her apparent innocence and purity as he contemplates her, together with his new-found knowledge of the evil the world contains, leads him to exclaim in a rush of desire to protect her: "Get thee to a nunnery." Later in the scene he discovers that Ophelia's father and his uncle, the murderous king, are both spying on this inter-view and infers, rightly, that Ophelia, with her prayerbook, has been planted here by them. In a frenzy of anger at her willingness to betray

him in this way, he associates her with all the vice of which he has so re-
cently learned that women can be guilty, and now cries again, "Get thee
to a nunnery." But the meaning this time is intensified by a pun. "Nun-
nery" was a slang term for a house of prostitution, and the punning use
of this sense along with the other sense sums up and dramatizes for us
Hamlet's anguish and bewilderment as he looks at her. If she is as inno-
cent as she seems in her manner and her speech, then a nunnery is the
place for her, to keep her from contamination in a vile world. But if she
is as corrupt as she seems in having betrayed him, and as corrupt as his
mother has proved to be, then a "nunnery"—in the base sense—is the
place for her. This pun, one of the most moving in literature, indicates
what meaning can be packed into a pun by one who knows how.


### iv

Study the examples of allusion and pun in the following poems:


[ 3 ]           *There Was an Old Man of Dunoon*
                        ANONYMOUS

>       There was an old man of Dunoon
>       Who always ate soup with a fork.
>           For he said: "As I eat
>           Neither fish, fowl, nor flesh,
>       I should otherwise finish too quick."          5


[ 4 ]                *Epitaph on Newton*
            ALEXANDER POPE (1688–1744)

>   Nature and Nature's laws lay hid in night:
>   God said, "Let Newton be!" and all was light.


## QUESTIONS

1 ★ The point of poem 3 comes from the fact that it alludes to a well-
    known kind of poem. What is the kind? How does this poem differ
    from the kind? If all poems of this kind came to be written like the

one above, would the kind be more or less interesting? What does your
conclusion indicate about the source of the main interest of the type?

2 ★ Poem 4 makes two allusions. What are they?

3 ★ There are puns in "night" and "light." Explain them.

[ 5 ]                    *On His Blindness*
                    JOHN MILTON (1608–1674)

When I consider how my light is spent
Ere half my days in this dark world and wide,
And that one talent° which is death to hide
Lodged with me useless, though my soul more bent
To serve therewith my Maker, and present                     5
My true account, lest He returning chide,
"Doth God exact day-labor, light denied?"
I fondly ask. But Patience, to prevent
That murmur, soon replies, "God doth not need
Either man's work or His own gifts.° Who best              10
Bear His mild yoke,° they serve Him best. His state
Is kingly: thousands° at His bidding speed,
And post o'er land and ocean without rest;
They also serve who only stand and wait." °

QUESTIONS

1 ★ In lines 1–8 Milton's speaker alludes to the New Testament parable of
    the talents. What is the speaker's own "talent"? Why does he fear it
    will now be "useless"?

---

°talent: See Matthew 25:14–30.    °His own gifts: the gifts God gives to
men.
°mild yoke: Christ says in Matthew 11:30, "... my yoke is easy, and my
burden is light."
°thousands: angels.
°They ... wait: The reference here is also to angels; those who "serve"
through meditation are of the highest order.

2 ★ Since "useless" has the double sense here of "not usable" and "not yielding interest" ("use" can mean a return on one's money, as in the parable of the talents), it is a pun. "Light" in line 7 and "wait" in line 14 are also puns. Explain each.

3 ★ What is compared to what by the metaphor in "spent" (line 1)? The metaphor in "exact day-labor" (line 7)? The metaphor in "yoke" (line 11)?

4 ★ In the first eight lines the words "I," "me," "my" appear frequently. In the last six, these are replaced by "He," "His," "Him." Relate this fact to the change that the poem traces in the speaker's attitude.

[ 6 ]    *On First Looking into Chapman's° Homer*
              JOHN KEATS (1795–1821)

Much have I traveled in the realms of gold,
    And many goodly states and kingdoms seen;
    Round many western islands have I been
Which bards in fealty to Apollo hold.
Oft of one wide expanse had I been told                          5
    That deep-browed Homer ruled as his demesne;
    Yet did I never breathe its pure serene
Till I heard Chapman speak out loud and bold:
Then felt I like some watcher of the skies
    When a new planet swims into his ken;                        10
Or like stout Cortez° when with eagle eyes
    He stared at the Pacific—and all his men
Looked at each other with a wild surmise—
    Silent, upon a peak in Darien.°

---

°**Chapman:** George Chapman, Elizabethan playwright and poet who translated Homer.
°**Cortez:** leader in Spain's New World conquests; historically, Balboa discovered the Pacific.
°**Darien:** Panama.

QUESTIONS

1 ★ The speaker has "traveled" to "realms of gold," "goodly states and kingdoms," and "western islands," all of which refer physically to Europe and the New World (the Age of Discovery) but metaphorically (and that is what counts) to the great works of literature that the speaker has read. How is the metaphor carried through in relation to Homer? Be specific. What form of discovery is involved here?

2 ★ What two activities are alluded to in the similes of the last six lines? How do these forms of discovery relate to the discovery dealt with in the first eight lines? How can it be said that the poem is developed around one major metaphor, with three different illustrations?

3 ★ What do the choices for comparison show about Keats's attitude toward literature in general, and his particular feelings on discovering Homer through Chapman's translation?

[ 7 ]                           *The Kingdom of God*
                               "In No Strange Land"

                    FRANCIS THOMPSON (1860–1907)

O world invisible, we view thee,
O world intangible, we touch thee,
O world unknowable, we know thee,
Inapprehensible, we clutch thee!

Does the fish soar to find the ocean,                                    5
The eagle plunge to find the air—
That we ask of the stars in motion
If they have rumor of thee there?

Not where the wheeling systems° darken,
And our benumbed conceiving soars!—                                     10

---

°**wheeling systems:** the galaxies.

The drift of pinions,° would we hearken,
Beats at our own clay-shuttered doors.

The angels keep their ancient places;
Turn but a stone, and start a wing!
'Tis ye, 'tis your estrangèd faces,                          15
That miss the many-splendored thing.

But, when so sad thou canst not sadder,
Cry;—and upon thy so sore loss
Shall shine the traffic of Jacob's ladder
Pitched betwixt Heaven and Charing Cross.°                   20

Yea, in the night, my Soul, my daughter,
Cry,—clinging Heaven by the hems;
And lo, Christ walking on the water
Not of Gennesareth,° but Thames!°

## QUESTIONS

1 ★ "Thee" in the first stanza refers, of course, to God. What paradoxes are raised in this stanza? How does the rest of the poem resolve them?

2 ★ Why are the questions in lines 5–6 raised? How do they serve to answer themselves, and by extension to answer the question posed in lines 7–8 and expanded on in the third and fourth stanzas? Where are the angels' "ancient places"?

3 ★ The title and subtitle allude to Luke 17:20–21 and Psalm 137:4. Line 19 alludes to Genesis 28:10–17; line 22 to Matthew 9:20–22 and 14:33–36; and lines 23–24 to Matthew 14:22–33. What part do these Biblical allusions play in the poem?

---

°pinions: wings.    °Charing Cross: section of London.    °Gennesareth:
Sea of Galilee.    °Thames: river that flows through London.

[ 8 ]                    *Kind of an Ode to Duty*
                        OGDEN NASH (1903–      )

O Duty,
Why hast thou not the visage of a sweetie or a cutie?
Why glitter thy spectacles so ominously?
Why art thou clad so abominously?
Why art thou so different from Venus                              5
And why do thou and I have so few interests mutually in common
    between us?
Why art thou fifty per cent martyr
And fifty-one per cent Tartar?

Why is it thy unfortunate wont
To try to attract people by calling on them either to leave undone
    the deeds they like, or to do the deeds they don't?               10
Why art thou so like an April postmortem
On something that died in the ortumn?
Above all, why dost thou continue to hound me?
Why are thou always albatrossly hanging around me?

Thou so ubiquitous,                                              15
And I so iniquitous.
I seem to be the one person in the world thou art perpetually
    preaching at who or to who;
Whatever looks like fun, there art thou standing between me and
    it, calling yoo-hoo.
O Duty, Duty!
How noble a man should I be hadst thou the visage of a sweetie
    or a cutie!                                                    20
But as it is thou art so much forbiddinger than a Wodehouse hero's
    forbiddingest aunt
That in the words of the poet, When Duty whispers low, Thou
    must, this erstwhile youth replies, I just can't.

## QUESTIONS

An *ode* is a relatively long, complex, and serious poem. There have been odes to and on all kinds of abstractions: dejection, adversity, solitude, indolence, melancholy, and, of course, duty. Nash is obviously alluding to William Wordsworth's "Ode to Duty" and to odes in general. The first stanza of Wordsworth's "Ode" goes like this:

> Stern Daughter of the Voice of God!
> O Duty! if that name thou love,
> Who art a light to guide, a rod
> To check the erring, and reprove;
> Thou, who art victory and law                                            5
> When empty terrors overawe;
> From vain temptations dost set free;
> And calm'st the weary strife of frail humanity!

> —From *Ode to Duty*
> WILLIAM WORDSWORTH (1770–1850)

In other stanzas in the poem Wordsworth calls Duty "Stern Lawgiver" and "awful Power," but says that she wears "the Godhead's most benignant grace" and that he does not know "anything so fair/As is the smile upon thy face." Wordsworth wants to "serve more strictly," to be Duty's "Bondman," so that he can live in a "repose that ever is the same."

The poet referred to in the last line of Nash's poem is Ralph Waldo Emerson. Part III of Emerson's poem "Voluntaries" ends:

> When Duty whispers low, *thou must,*
> The youth replies, *I can.*

1 ★ Nash's poem can be enjoyed without any knowledge of the foregoing information, but what does it gain by the allusions to the ode form itself and to Wordsworth's and Emerson's poems? What is the allusion in line 14 and how does it add to the poem's meaning? What is the pun in the phrase "hanging around"?

2 ★ Why does the speaker wish Duty had the "visage of a sweetie or a cutie"? Why is "visage" a better word choice than "face" would be? (Look up the two words in a good dictionary; what special meaning does "visage" have?) What does Duty look like in this poem? What do you suppose "a Wodehouse hero's forbiddingest aunt" looks and acts

like? (P. G. Wodehouse is a modern British writer of humorous novels.)

3 ★ Why does the speaker use such words as "hast thou" and "art"? What other language forms echo old-fashioned diction? With what do these words obviously contrast?

4 ★ Why should this rightly be called a poem?

[ 9 ]                        *Journey of the Magi*°
                          T. S. ELIOT (1888–1965)

"A cold coming we had of it,
Just the worst time of the year
For a journey, and such a long journey:
The ways deep and the weather sharp,
The very dead of winter." °                                          5
And the camels galled, sore-footed, refractory,
Lying down in the melting snow.
There were times we regretted
The summer palaces on slopes, the terraces,
And the silken girls bringing sherbet.                               10
Then the camel men cursing and grumbling
And running away, and wanting their liquor and women,
And the night-fires going out, and the lack of shelters,
And the cities hostile and the towns unfriendly
And the villages dirty and charging high prices:                    15
A hard time we had of it.
At the end we preferred to travel all night,
Sleeping in snatches,

---

°**Title:** See Matthew 2.
°**Lines 1–5:** The lines in quotation marks are adapted from a sermon by Bishop Lancelot Andrewes on Christmas Day, 1622: "It was no summer progress. A cold coming they had of it at this time of the year, just the worst time of the year to take a journey, and specially a long journey, in. The ways deep, the weather sharp, the days short, the sun farthest off, ... the very dead of winter."

With the voices singing in our ears, saying
That this was all folly.                                            20

Then at dawn we came down to a temperate valley,
Wet, below the snow line, smelling of vegetation;
With a running stream and a watermill beating the darkness,
And three trees° on the low sky,
And an old white horse° galloped away in the meadow.               25
Then we came to a tavern with vine-leaves over the lintel,
Six hands at the open door dicing for pieces of silver,°
And feet kicking the empty wine-skins.
But there was no information, and so we continued
And arrived at evening, not a moment too soon                      30
Finding the place; it was (you may say) satisfactory.

All this was a long time ago, I remember,
And I would do it again, but set down
This set down
This: were we led all that way for                                 35
Birth or Death? There was a Birth, certainly,
We had evidence and no doubt. I had seen birth and death,
But had thought they were different; this Birth was
Hard and bitter agony for us, like Death, our death.
We returned to our places, these Kingdoms,                         40
But no longer at ease here, in the old dispensation,
With an alien people clutching their gods.
I should be glad of another death.

---

°**three trees:** alludes to the three "trees" on Calvary.
°**white horse:** Revelation 6:2—"And I saw, and beheld a white horse: and
he that sat on him had a bow; and a crown was given unto him; and he
went forth conquering, and to conquer." See also Revelation 19:11–14.
°**dicing . . . silver:** reference to the casting of lots for Jesus's garments and
his betrayal for "thirty pieces of silver."

## QUESTIONS

1 ★ What is the "subject" of this poem? Who are the Magi? What was their destination on this journey? What conditions did they meet with during its first phase (lines 1–20)? During its second phase (lines 21–31)? Why do you think the poet omits most of the third phase— the events surrounding their arrival? What was the effect on them when they returned home?

2 ★ Who is the speaker of the poem? How far is he a well-defined personality, how far a voice? What do you take to be the situation he is responding to? What is his audience? Do you think he is talking to someone, writing to someone, or simply going over the experience in his mind? How would you describe the speaker's tone?

3 ★ What type of foot recurs most frequently in the poem's rhythm? Does the poem have any recurrent sound pattern that functions in place of rhymes? What is it? To what extent does the rhythm of the third section combine the dominant rhythms of sections one and two?

4 ★ a. At the climax of the journey (line 31) the poet uses understatement. Explain.

   b. What paradox having to do with birth and death appears in the poem's third section (lines 32–43)? What paradox having to do with being homeless at home?

   c. In the second section the speaker describes certain things that for him are only scenes remembered from the journey, but for us are Christian symbols—the three trees, the white horse, pieces of silver, the dicing. This is a form of irony. What form? Do you find irony of any sort elsewhere in the poem?

   d. What use is made of allusion in the poem?

5 ★ Is the journey described in the poem simply a literal journey or is it a metaphor for something else? Could the two types of country the Magi go through represent kinds of experience which one must pass through but not linger in if one wishes to discover the Birth?

6 ★ The journey's upshot is obviously discomfort after the return home. Then why does the speaker say he would do it again? Does the poem suggest there may be something wrong in being comfortable?

# V
# ADDITIONAL POEMS
# CHRONOLOGICALLY
# ARRANGED

Here are fifty-three poems, arranged chronologically to cover some four hundred years of English and American poetry, and divided roughly between the premodern and modern periods. Lines from many of these poems have been used for illustrative purposes in previous sections of the book.

We have attempted to offer a wide range of poetry in this section. We hope that our choices will underscore those aspects of poetry examined earlier in the book. Although they vary in subject, treatment, and difficulty, they have in common readability and excellence.

## The premodern period

### The Three Ravens
#### ANONYMOUS

There were three ravens sat on a tree,
Downe a downe, hay downe, hay downe.

There were three ravens sat on a tree,
   With a downe.
There were three ravens sat on a tree,          5
They were as blacke as they might be.
   With a downe derrie, derrie, derrie, downe, downe.

The one of them said to his mate,
"Where shall we our breakfast take?"

"Downe in yonder greene field,          10
There lies a knight slain under his shield.

"His hounds they lie downe at his feete,
So well they can their master keepe.

"His haukes they flie so eagerly,
There's no fowle dare him come nie." °        15

Downe there comes a fallow doe,°
As great with yong as she might goe.

She lift up his bloudy hed,
And kist his wounds that were so red.

She got him up upon her backe,         20
And carried him to earthen lake.°

She buried him before the prime,°
She was dead herselfe ere evensong° time.

God send every gentleman,
Such haukes, such hounds, and such a leman.°   25

---

°nie: nigh, near.   °fallow doe: See line 25.   °lake: pit.   °prime: early
morning worship.   °evensong: vespers; evening worship.   °leman:
sweetheart.

## Sonnet 94
### WILLIAM SHAKESPEARE (1564–1616)

They that have power to hurt and will do none,
That do not do the thing they most do show,°
Who, moving others, are themselves as stone,
Unmovèd, cold, and to temptation slow—
They rightly do inherit Heaven's graces                    5
And husband nature's riches from expense.°
They are the lords and owners of their faces,
Others but stewards° of their excellence.
The summer's flower is to the summer sweet,
Though to itself it only live and die,                     10
But if that flower with base infection meet,
The basest weed outbraves his dignity.°
    For sweetest things turn sourest by their deeds;
    Lilies that fester smell far worse than weeds.

## "Blow, Blow, Thou Winter Wind"
### From As You Like It, II, vii
### WILLIAM SHAKESPEARE (1564–1616)

Blow, blow, thou winter wind.
Thou are not so unkind
    As man's ingratitude.
Thy tooth is not so keen,
Because thou art not seen,                                 5
    Although thy breath be rude.
Heigh-ho! Sing, heigh-ho! unto the green holly.
Most friendship is feigning, most loving mere folly.
    Then, heigh-ho, the holly!
        This life is most jolly.                  10
    Freeze, freeze, thou bitter sky,
    That dost not bite so nigh

---

°**show:** show as possible.   °**expense:** wasteful use.   °**stewards:** servants, as opposed to "lords and owners."   °**outbraves ... dignity:** outdoes the flower.

As benefits forgot.
Though thou the waters warp,
Thy sting is not so sharp                              15
As friend remembered not.
Heigh-ho! Sing, heigh-ho! unto the green holly.
Most friendship is feigning, most loving mere folly.
Then, heigh-ho, the holly!
This life is most jolly.                               20

## Go and Catch a Falling Star
JOHN DONNE (1572–1631)

Go and catch a falling star,
Get with child a mandrake° root,
Tell me where all past years are,
Or who cleft the devil's foot,
Teach me to hear mermaids° singing,                    5
Or to keep off envy's stinging,
And find
What wind
Serves t' advance an honest° mind.

If thou be'st born to strange sights,                  10
Things invisible to see,
Ride ten thousand days and nights
Till age snow° white hairs on thee;
Thou, when thou return'st, wilt tell me
All strange wonders that befell thee,                  15
And swear
Nowhere
Lives a woman true, and fair.

If thou find'st one, let me know;
Such a pilgrimage were sweet;                          20

---

°**mandrake:** an herb whose forked root resembles the human form.   °**mer-
maids:**   the sirens.   °**honest:** chaste.   °**snow:** here a verb.

Yet do not, I would not go
    Though at next door we might meet.
Though she were true when you met her,
And last till you write your letter,
        Yet she                                                    25
        Will be
False ere I come, to two or three.


## A Hymn to God the Father
### JOHN DONNE (1572–1631)

Wilt Thou forgive that sin where I begun,
    Which was my sin, though it were done before?
Wilt Thou forgive that sin, through which I run,
    And do run still, though still I do deplore?
        When Thou hast done, Thou hast not done,°        5
        For I have more.

Wilt Thou forgive that sin which I have won
    Others to sin, and made my sin their door?
Wilt Thou forgive that sin which I did shun
    A year, or two: but wallowed in a score?            10
        When Thou hast done, Thou hast not done,
        For I have more.

I have a sin of fear, that when I have spun
    My last thread, I shall perish on the shore;°
But swear by Thy self, that at my death Thy Son        15
    Shall shine as He shines now, and heretofore;
        And, having done that, Thou hast done;
        I fear no more.

---

°**done:** a pun on the poet's name.    °**perish . . . shore:** have no afterlife.

## Still to Be Neat

BEN JONSON (1572–1637)

Still to be neat, still to be dressed  
As° you were going to a feast;  
Still to be powdered, still perfumed:  
Lady, it is to be presumed,  
Though art's hid causes are not found,                        5  
All is not sweet, all is not sound.  

Give me a look, give me a face  
That makes simplicity a grace;  
Robes loosely flowing, hair as free:  
Such sweet neglect more taketh me                            10  
Than all th' adulteries of art;  
They strike mine eyes, but not my heart.  

## Love

GEORGE HERBERT (1593–1633)

Love bade me welcome, yet my soul drew back,  
    Guilty of dust and sin.  
But quick-eyed Love, observing me grow slack  
    From my first entrance in,  
Drew nearer to me, sweetly questioning                       5  
    If I lacked anything.  

A guest, I answered, worthy to be here.  
    Love said, You shall be he.  
I, the unkind, the ungrateful? Ah, my dear,  
    I cannot look on thee.                            10  
Love took my hand and smiling did reply,  
    Who made the eyes but I?  

---

°**as:** as if.

Truth, Lord, but I have marred them; let my shame
   Go where it doth deserve.
And know you not, says Love, who bore the blame?    15
   My dear, then I will serve.
You must sit down, says Love, and taste my meat.
   So I did sit and eat.


## The Pulley°

### GEORGE HERBERT (1593–1633)

When God at first made man,
Having a glass of blessings standing by,
Let us, said he, pour on him all we can.
Let the world's riches, which dispersèd lie,
   Contract into a span.    5

So strength first made a way,
Then beauty flowed, then wisdom, honor, pleasure.
When almost all was out, God made a stay,
Perceiving that alone of all his treasure
   Rest in the bottom lay.    10

For if I should, said he,
Bestow this jewel also on my creature,
He would adore my gifts instead of me,
And rest in nature, not the God of nature;
   So both should losers be.    15

Yet let him keep the rest,
But keep them with repining restlessness.
Let him be rich and weary, that at least,
If goodness lead him not, yet weariness
   May toss him to my breast.    20

---

°**Title:** Be sure you know what a pulley is used for.

## *Go, Lovely Rose*
EDMUND WALLER (1606–1687)

Go, lovely rose!
Tell her that wastes her time and me
   That now she knows,
When I resemble her to thee,
   How sweet and fair she seems to be.     5

Tell her that's young
And shuns to have her graces spied,
   That hadst thou sprung
In deserts where no men abide,
   Thou must have uncommended died.     10

Small is the worth
Of beauty from the light retired:
   Bid her come forth,
Suffer her self to be desired,
   And not blush so to be admired.     15

Then die, that she
The common fate of all things rare
   May read in thee,
How small a part of time they share,
   That are so wondrous sweet and fair.     20

## *Why So Pale and Wan*
SIR JOHN SUCKLING (1609–1642)

Why so pale and wan, fond lover?
   Prithee, why so pale?
Will, when looking well can't move her,
   Looking ill prevail?
   Prithee, why so pale?     5

Why so dull and mute, young sinner?
　　Prithee, why so mute?
Will, when speaking well can't win her,
　　Saying nothing do 't?
　　Prithee, why so mute?　　　　　　　　　　10

Quit, quit, for shame, this will not move,
　　This cannot take her.
If of herself she will not love,
　　Nothing can make her.
　　The devil take her!　　　　　　　　　　15


## To Lucasta, Going to the Wars

RICHARD LOVELACE (1618–1658)

Tell me not, sweet, I am unkind,
　　That from the nunnery
Of thy chaste breast and quiet mind,
　　To war and arms I fly.

True, a new mistress now I chase,　　　　5
　　The first foe in the field;
And with a stronger faith embrace
　　A sword, a horse, a shield.

Yet this inconstancy is such
　　As you too shall adore;　　　　　　　10
I could not love thee, Dear, so much,
　　Loved I not honor more.


## To His Coy Mistress

ANDREW MARVELL (1621–1678)

Had we but world enough, and time,
This coyness, Lady, were no crime.

We would sit down, and think which way
To walk, and pass our long love's day.
Thou by the Indian Ganges' side                    5
Shouldst rubies find: I by the tide
Of Humber° would complain. I would
Love you ten years before the Flood:
And you should, if you please, refuse
Till the conversion of the Jews.                   10
My vegetable° love should grow
Vaster than empires, and more slow.
An hundred years should go to praise
Thine eyes, and on thy forehead gaze.
Two hundred to adore each breast:                  15
But thirty thousand to the rest.
An age at least to every part,
And the last age should show your heart.
For, Lady, you deserve this state;°
Nor would I love at lower rate.°                    20
     But at my back I always hear
Time's wingèd chariot hurrying near:
And yonder all before us lie
Deserts of vast eternity.
Thy beauty shall no more be found,                 25
Nor, in thy marble vault, shall sound
My echoing song: then worms shall try°
That long preserved virginity:
And your quaint° honor turn to dust,
And into ashes all my lust.                        30
The grave's a fine and private place,
But none, I think, do there embrace.
     Now therefore, while the youthful hue
Sits on thy skin like morning dew,

---

°**Humber:** estuary of the Trent and Ouse Rivers on the east coast of England,
the site of Hull, the city in which the poet lived.    °**vegetable:** growing;
alive.    °**state:** royal treatment.    °**lower rate:** reference to value or cost.
°**try:** attempt (successfully).    °**quaint:** prudish; old-maidish.

And while thy willing soul transpires°                    35
At every pore with instant° fires,
Now let us sport us while we may;
And now, like am'rous birds of prey,
Rather at once our time devour,
Than languish in his slow-chapped° power.                 40
Let us roll all our strength, and all
Our sweetness, up into one ball:
And tear our pleasures with rough strife,
Through the iron gates of life.
Thus, though we cannot make our sun                       45
Stand still, yet we will make him run.

## Ode on Solitude

ALEXANDER POPE (1688–1744)

Happy the man, whose wish and care
    A few paternal acres bound,
Content to breathe his native an,
        In his own ground.

Whose herds with milk, whose fields with bread,           5
    Whose flocks supply him with attire,
Whose trees in summer yield him shade,
        In winter fire.

Blest, who can unconcern'dly find
    Hours, days, and years slide soft away,               10
In health of body, peace of mind,
        Quiet by day,

Sound sleep by night; study and ease,
    Together mixed; sweet recreation;
And innocence, which most does please                     15
        With meditation.

---

°**transpires**: breathes.    °**instant**: eager.    °**slow-chapped**: slow-jawed;
slow-devouring.

Thus let me live, unseen, unknown,
　　Thus unlamented let me die,
Steal from the world, and not a stone
　　　　Tell where I lie.                    20


## To a Young Heir

SAMUEL JOHNSON (1709–1784)

Long-expected one-and-twenty,
　　Ling'ring year, at length is flown:
Pride and pleasure, pomp and plenty,
　　Great * * * * * * *, are now your own.

Loosened from the minor's tether,                    5
　　Free to mortgage or to sell,
Wild as wind, and light as feather,
　　Bid the sons of thrift farewell.

Call the Betsies, Kates, and Jennies,
　　All the names that banish care;              10
Lavish of your grandsire's guineas,°
　　Show the spirit of an heir.

All that prey on vice and folly
　　Joy to see their quarry fly:
There the gamester, light and jolly,              15
　　There the lender, grave and sly.

Wealth, my lad, was made to wander,
　　Let it wander as it will;
Call the jockey,° call the pander,
　　Bid them come and take their fill.              20

---

°**guineas:** coins now worth about $3.　　°**jockey:** swindler.

When the bonny blade carouses,
   Pockets full, and spirits high—
What are acres? What are houses?
   Only dirt, or° wet or dry.

Should the guardian friend or mother                    25
   Tell the woes of willful waste,
Scorn their counsel, scorn their pother;—°
   You can hang or drown at last!

## The Tiger

WILLIAM BLAKE (1757–1827)

Tiger, Tiger, burning bright
In the forests of the night,
What immortal hand or eye
Could frame thy fearful symmetry?

In what distant deeps or skies                          5
Burnt the fire of thine eyes?
On what wings dare he aspire?
What the hand dare seize the fire?

And what shoulder, and what art,
Could twist the sinews of thy heart?                    10
And when thy heart began to beat,
What dread hand and what dread feet?

What the hammer? What the chain?
In what furnace was thy brain?
What the anvil? What dread grasp                        15
Dare its deadly terrors clasp?

When the stars threw down their spears,
And watered heaven with their tears,

---

°or: either.  °pother: fussing.

Did He smile His work to see?
Did He who made the lamb make thee? 20

Tiger, Tiger, burning bright
In the forests of the night,
What immortal hand or eye
Dare frame thy fearful symmetry?

## Mock On, Mock On, Voltaire, Rousseau
WILLIAM BLAKE (1757–1827)

Mock on, mock on, Voltaire,° Rousseau:°
Mock on, mock on; 'tis all in vain!
You throw the sand against the wind,
And the wind blows it back again.

And every sand becomes a gem 5
Reflected in the beams divine;
Blown back, they blind the mocking eye,
But still in Israel's paths they shine.

The atoms of Democritus°
And Newton's° particles of light 10
Are sands upon the Red Sea shore,
Where Israel's tents do shine so bright.

---

°**Voltaire:** pen name of François Marie Arouet (1694–1778), French philosopher and writer. All four men mentioned in the poem were, in Blake's eyes, debunkers of faith or the spirit, as symbolized by the Israelites whom God delivered out of bondage in Egypt (see the "Red Sea" reference in line 11).

°**Rousseau:** Jean Jacques Rousseau (1712–1778), French philosopher and writer.

°**Democritus:** Greek scientific philosopher (460?–357? B.C.), who developed one theory of atom behavior.

°**Newton:** Sir Isaac Newton (1642–1727), English scientific philosopher, originator of the particle theory of light.

## A Poison Tree
WILLIAM BLAKE (1757–1827)

I was angry with my friend:
I told my wrath, my wrath did end.
I was angry with my foe:
I told it not, my wrath did grow.

And I watered it in fears,                                    5
Night and morning with my tears:
And I sunnèd it with smiles,
And with soft deceitful wiles.

And it grew both day and night,
Till it bore an apple bright;                                 10
And my foe beheld it shine,
And he knew that it was mine,

And into my garden stole
When the night had veiled the pole:
In the morning glad I see                                     15
My foe outstretched beneath the tree.

## And Did Those Feet in Ancient Time
WILLIAM BLAKE (1757–1827)

And did those feet in ancient time
Walk upon England's mountains green?°
And was the holy Lamb of God
On England's pleasant pastures seen?

And did the Countenance Divine                               5
Shine forth upon our clouded hills?

---

°And did . . . mountains green: see Isaiah, 52:7.

And was Jerusalem builded here
Among these dark Satanic Mills?°

Bring me my Bow of burning gold:
Bring me my Arrows of desire:                          10
Bring me my Spear: O clouds unfold!
Bring me my Chariot of fire.

I will not cease from Mental Fight,
Nor shall my Sword sleep in my hand
Till we have built Jerusalem°                          15
In England's green and pleasant Land.

## My Luve Is Like a Red, Red Rose
### ROBERT BURNS (1759–1796)

O, my luve is like a red, red rose,
    That's newly sprung in June.
O my luve is like the melodie
    That's sweetly played in tune.

As fair art thou, my bonnie lass,                      5
    So deep in luve am I,
And I will luve thee still, my dear,
    Till a'° the seas gang° dry.

Till a' the seas gang dry, my dear,
    And the rocks melt wi' the sun!                  10
And I will luve thee still, my dear,
    While the sands o' life shall run.

---

°**Satanic Mills:** probably a reference to the grimy, inhuman factories of the early years of the Industrial Revolution.   °**Jerusalem:** i.e., the "New Jerusalem" of Biblical prophetic writing: the City of God on earth.   °**a':** all.   °**gang:** go.

And fare thee weel,° my only luve,
    And fare thee weel awhile!
And I will come again, my luve,                          15
    Though it were ten thousand mile!


## She Dwelt Among the Untrodden Ways
### WILLIAM WORDSWORTH (1770–1850)

She dwelt among the untrodden ways
    Beside the springs of Dove,
A Maid whom there were none to praise
    And very few to love:

A violet by a mossy stone                                5
    Half hidden from the eye!
—Fair as a star, when only one
    Is shining in the sky.

She lived unknown, and few could know
    When Lucy ceased to be;                          10
But she is in her grave, and, oh,
    The difference to me!


## A Slumber Did My Spirit Seal
### WILLIAM WORDSWORTH (1770–1850)

A slumber did my spirit seal;
    I had no human fears:
She seemed a thing that could not feel
    The touch of earthly years.

---

°weel: well.

No motion has she now, no force;                          5
   She neither hears nor sees;
Rolled round in earth's diurnal° course,
   With rocks, and stones, and trees.

## The World Is Too Much With Us
### WILLIAM WORDSWORTH (1770–1850)

The world is too much with us; late and soon,
Getting and spending, we lay waste our powers:
Little we see in Nature that is ours;
We have given our hearts away, a sordid boon!
This Sea that bares her bosom to the moon;                5
The winds that will be howling at all hours,
And are up-gathered now like sleeping flowers;
For this, for everything, we are out of tune;
It moves us not.—Great God! I'd rather be
A pagan suckled in a creed outworn;                      10
So might I, standing on this pleasant lea,
Have glimpses that would make me less forlorn;
Have sight of Proteus° rising from the sea;
Or hear old Triton° blow his wreathèd horn.

---

°**diurnal:** daily.
°**Proteus:** Greek sea god, herdsman for Poseidon (Neptune). Proteus could
change shape whenever he wished.
°**Triton:** another Greek sea god, son of Poseidon; he controlled the waves
with his "wreathèd horn" (conch shell).

## *Kubla Khan*

SAMUEL TAYLOR COLERIDGE (1772–1834)

In Xanadu° did Kubla Khan
   A stately pleasure-dome decree;
Where Alph, the sacred river, ran
   Through caverns measureless to man
Down to a sunless sea.                      5
So twice five miles of fertile ground
With walls and towers were girdled round;
And here were gardens bright with sinuous rills
Where blossomed many an incense-bearing tree;
And here were forests ancient as the hills,       10
Enfolding sunny spots of greenery.

But O, that deep romantic chasm which slanted
Down the green hill athwart a cedarn cover!
A savage place! as holy and enchanted
As e'er beneath a waning moon was haunted     15
By woman wailing for her demon-lover!
And from this chasm, with ceaseless turmoil seething,
As if this earth in fast thick pants were breathing,
A mighty fountain momently was forced;
Amid whose swift, half-intermitted burst       20
Huge fragments vaulted like rebounding hail,
Or chaffy grain beneath the thresher's flail.

---

°**Xanadu:** As with "the sacred river" Alph (line 3), this is no real place, but simply any remote, exotic spot where the great Mongol emperor, Kubla Khan, could "decree" that a magnificent palace be built. The first 36 lines of the poem describe the wonder of Kubla Khan's "paradise" and the geyser that "momently" brings the sacred river to the surface. The last 18 lines play off against the first 36: the speaker ("I") will build a more magnificent "pleasure-dome" in the form of his artistic creation.

And 'mid these dancing rocks at once and ever
It flung up momently the sacred river.
Five miles meandering with a mazy motion 25
Through wood and dale the sacred river ran,
Then reached the caverns measureless to man,
And sank in tumult to a lifeless ocean;
And 'mid this tumult Kubla heard from far
Ancestral voices prophesying war! 30

    The shadow of the dome of pleasure
        Floated midway on the waves;
    Where was heard the mingled measure
        From the fountain and the caves.
It was a miracle of rare device, 35
A sunny pleasure-dome with caves of ice!

    A damsel with a dulcimer
        In a vision once I saw.
    It was an Abyssinian maid,
        And on her dulcimer she played, 40
Singing of Mount Abora.
Could I revive within me
    Her symphony and song,
To such a deep delight 'twould win me
That with music loud and long, 45
I would build that dome in air,
That sunny dome! those caves of ice!
And all who heard should see them there,
And all should cry, Beware! Beware!
His flashing eyes, his floating hair! 50
Weave a circle round him thrice,
    And close your eyes with holy dread,
    For he on honey-dew hath fed,
And drunk the milk of Paradise.

## *To Autumn*
### JOHN KEATS (1795–1821)

### I

Season of mists and mellow fruitfulness,
    Close bosom-friend of the maturing sun;
Conspiring with him how to load and bless
    With fruit the vines that round the thatch-eaves run;
To bend with apples the mossed cottage-trees,                    5
    And fill all fruit with ripeness to the core;
        To swell the gourd, and plump the hazel shells
    With a sweet kernel; to set budding more,
And still more, later flowers for the bees,
Until they think warm days will never cease,                     10
        For Summer has o'er-brimmed their clammy° cells.

### II

Who hath not seen thee oft amid thy store?
    Sometimes whoever seeks abroad may find
Thee sitting careless on a granary floor,
    Thy hair soft-lifted by the winnowing wind;                    15
Or on a half-reaped furrow sound asleep,
    Drowsed with the fume of poppies, while thy hook°
        Spares the next swath and all its twinèd flowers:
And sometimes like a gleaner thou dost keep
    Steady thy laden head across a brook;                          20
    Or by a cider-press, with patient look,
        Thou watchest the last oozings hours by hours.

### III

Where are the songs of Spring? Ay, where are they?
    Think not of them, thou hast thy music too,—
While barrèd clouds bloom the soft-dying day,                    25
    And touch the stubble-plains with rosy hue;

---

°**clammy:** moist and sticky.   °**hook:** scythe.

Then in a wailful choir the small gnats mourn
   Among the river sallows,° borne aloft
   Or sinking as the light wind lives or dies;
And full-grown lambs loud bleat from hilly bourn;°      30
   Hedge-crickets sing; and now with treble° soft
   The red-breast whistles from a garden-croft;°
   And gathering swallows twitter in the skies.

## Ode on a Grecian Urn

JOHN KEATS (1795–1821)

Thou° still unravished bride of quietness,
   Thou foster-child of silence and slow time,
Sylvan historian, who canst thus express°
   A flowery tale more sweetly than our rhyme:
What leaf-fringed legend haunts about thy shape     5
   Of deities or mortals, or of both,
      In Tempe or the dales of Arcady?°
What men or gods are these? What maidens loth?
   What mad pursuit? What struggle to escape?
      What pipes and timbrels?° What wild ectasy?   10

Heard melodies are sweet, but those unheard°
   Are sweeter; therefore, ye soft pipes, play on;
Not to the sensual ear, but, more endeared,
   Pipe to the spirit ditties of no tone:
Fair youth, beneath the trees, thou canst not leave   15
   Thy song, nor ever can those trees be bare;
      Bold Lover, never, never canst thou kiss,
Though winning near the goal—yet, do not grieve;
   She cannot fade, though thou hast not thy bliss,
      For ever wilt thou love, and she be fair!   20

---

°sallows: willows.   °bourn: small stream.   °treble: high-pitched sound.
°croft: small, enclosed field.   °Thou . . .; the speaker is addressing the
decorated urn; the references in the poem reveal what is pictured on it.
°express: tell.   °Tempe . . . Arcady: valleys in Greece, highly idealized.
°timbrels: tambourines.   °unheard: i.e., imagined.

Ah, happy, happy boughs! that cannot shed
    Your leaves, nor ever bid the spring adieu;
And, happy melodist, unwearièd,
    For ever piping songs for ever new;
More happy love! more happy, happy love!        25
    For ever warm and still to be enjoyed,
        For ever panting, and for ever young;
All breathing human passion far above,
    That leaves a heart high-sorrowful and cloyed,
        A burning forehead, and a parching tongue.    30

Who are these coming to the sacrifice?
    To what green altar, O mysterious priest,
Lead'st thou that heifer lowing at the skies,
    And all her silken flanks with garlands dressed?
What little town by river or sea shore,        35
    Or mountain-built with peaceful citadel,
        Is emptied of this folk, this pious morn?
And, little town, thy streets for evermore
    Will silent be; and not a soul to tell
        Why thou art desolate, can e'er return.    40

O Attic° shape! Fair attitude! with brede°
    Of marble men and maidens overwrought,
With forest branches and the trodden weed;
    Thou, silent form, dost tease us out of thought
As doth eternity:° Cold Pastoral!        45
    When old age shall this generation waste,
        Thou shalt remain, in midst of other woe
Than ours, a friend to man, to whom thou say'st,
    "Beauty is truth, truth beauty,"—that is all
        Ye know on earth, and all ye need to know.    50

---

°**Attic:** region of Greece; Athens was its capital.    °**brede:** embroidery,
ornamentation.    °**eternity:** i.e., the idea of eternity.

## *Dover Beach*

MATTHEW ARNOLD (1822–1888)

The sea is calm tonight,
The tide is full, the moon lies fair
Upon the Straits;—on the French coast, the light
Gleams, and is gone; the cliffs of England° stand,
Glimmering and vast, out in the tranquil bay.                    5
Come to the window, sweet is the night air!
Only, from the long line of spray
Where the sea meets the moon-blanched sand,
Listen! you hear the grating roar
Of pebbles which the waves suck back, and fling,                10
At their return, up the high strand,
Begin, and cease, and then again begin,
With tremulous cadence slow, and bring
The eternal note of sadness in.

Sophocles° long ago                                            15
Heard it on the Aegean, and it brought
Into his mind the turbid ebb and flow
Of human misery; we
Find also in the sound a thought,
Hearing it by this distant northern sea.                       20

The sea of faith
Was once, too, at the full, and round earth's shore
Lay like the folds of a bright girdle° furled;
But now I only hear
Its melancholy, long, withdrawing roar,                        25

---

°**cliffs of England:** the Dover chalk cliffs.
°**Sophocles:** Greek dramatist; in *Antigone* he has the chorus associate man's
lot with "a wave cresting out of the black northeast,/When the long dark-
ness under sea roars up/And bursts drumming death upon the wind-
whipped sand." (Translation of Dudley Fitts and Robert Fitzgerald.)
°**girdle:** sash.

Retreating to the breath
Of the night-wind down the vast edges drear
And naked shingles° of the world.

  Ah, love, let us be true
To one another! for the world, which seems                    30
To lie before us like a land of dreams,
So various, so beautiful, so new,
Hath really neither joy, nor love, nor light,
Nor certitude, nor peace, nor help for pain;
And we are here as on a darkling plain                        35
Swept with confused alarms of struggle and flight,
Where ignorant armies clash by night.


**The modern period**


### I Like to See It Lap the Miles
EMILY DICKINSON (1830–1886)

I like to see it lap the miles,
And lick the valleys up,
And stop to feed itself at tanks;
And then, prodigious, step

Around a pile of mountains,                                   5
And, supercilious, peer
In shanties by the sides of roads;
And then a quarry pare

To fit its ribs, and crawl between,
Complaining all the while                                     10
In horrid, hooting stanza;
Then chase itself down hill

---

°shingles: gravel beaches.

And neigh like Boanerges;°
Then, punctual as a star,
Stop—docile and omnipotent—                    15
At its own stable door.


## I Heard a Fly Buzz When I Died
### EMILY DICKINSON (1830–1886)

I heard a fly buzz when I died;
The stillness in the room
Was like the stillness in the air
Between the heaves of storm.

The eyes around had wrung them dry,          5
And breaths were gathering firm
For that last onset, when the king
Be witnessed in the room.

I willed my keepsakes, signed away
What portion of me be                          10
Assignable,—and then it was
There interposed a fly,

With blue, uncertain, stumbling buzz,
Between the light and me;
And then the windows failed, and then         15
I could not see to see.


## After Great Pain a Formal Feeling Comes
### EMILY DICKINSON (1830–1886)

After great pain a formal feeling comes—
The nerves sit ceremonious like tombs;

---

°**Boanerges:** "sons of thunder," name applied by Jesus to the sons of Zebe-
dee, James and John, who wanted to destroy the Samaritans with fire from
heaven.

The stiff heart questions—was it He that bore?
And yesterday—or centuries before?

The feet mechanical go round                              5
A wooden way
Of ground or air or ought,
Regardless grown,
A quartz contentment like a stone.

This is the hour of lead                                  10
Remembered if outlived
As freezing persons recollect
The snow—
First chill, then stupor, then
The letting go.                                          15

## God's Grandeur

GERARD MANLEY HOPKINS (1844–1889)

The world is charged with the grandeur of God.
    It will flame out, like shining from shook foil;°
    It gathers to a greatness, like the ooze of oil°
Crushed. Why do men then now not reck his rod?°
Generations have trod, have trod, have trod;             5
    And all is seared with trade; bleared, smeared with toil;
    And wears man's smudge and shares man's smell: the soil
Is bare now, nor can foot feel, being shod.

And for° all this, nature is never spent;°
    There lives the dearest freshness deep down things;   10
And though the last lights off the black West went
    Oh, morning, at the brown brink eastward, springs—
Because the Holy Ghost over the bent
    World broods with warm breast and with ah! bright wings.

---

°foil: thin sheetmetal.    °ooze of oil: from pressed olives.    °reck his rod:
concern themselves about God's punishment.    °for: in spite of.    °spent:
used up; exhausted.

## *Spring and Fall:*
### To a Young Child

GERARD MANLEY HOPKINS (1844–1889)

Márgarét,° are you griéving
Over Goldengrove unleaving?°
Leáves, líke the things of man, you
With your fresh thoughts care for, can you?
Áh! Ás the heart grows older                              5
It will come to such sights colder
By and by, nor spare a sigh
Though worlds of wanwood leafmeal° lie;
And yet you wíll weep and know why.
Now no matter, child, the name:                          10
Sórrow's spríngs áre the same.
Nor mouth had, no nor mind, expressed
What heart heard of, ghost guessed:
It ís the blight man was born for,
It is Margaret you mourn for.                            15

## *Thou Art Indeed Just, Lord°*

GERARD MANLEY HOPKINS (1844–1889)

Justus quidem tu es, Domine, si disputem tecum: verum-tamen justa
loquar ad te: Quare via impiorum prosperatur? &c.

Thou art indeed just, Lord, if I contend
With thee; but, sir, so what I plead is just.
Why do sinners' ways prosper? and why must
Disappointment all I endeavour end?
Wert thou my enemy, O thou my friend,                    5
How wouldst thou worse, I wonder, than thou dost
Defeat, thwart me? Oh, the sots and thralls of lust

---

°**Márgarét:** The special stress marks are Hopkins's. Some syllables that
would not normally get stress are purposely given stress.
°**unleaving:** losing its leaves.     °**leafmeal:** like "piecemeal."
°**Title:** Jeremiah 12:1; the first three lines of the poem provide the transla-
tion for the Latin.

Do in spare hours more thrive than I that spend,
Sir, life upon thy cause. See, banks and brakes
Now, leavèd how thick! lacèd they are again                    10
With fretty chervil, look, and fresh wind shakes
Them; birds build—but not I build; no, but strain,
Time's eunuch, and not breed one work that wakes.
Mine, O thou lord of life, send my roots rain.


## On Wenlock Edge°

### A. E. HOUSMAN (1859–1936)

On Wenlock Edge the wood's in trouble;
    His forest fleece the Wrekin heaves;
The gale, it plies the saplings double,
    And thick on Severn snow the leaves.

'Twould blow like this through holt° and hanger°          5
    When Uricon the city stood:
'Tis the old wind in the old anger,
    But then it threshed another wood.

Then, 'twas before my time, the Roman
    At yonder heaving hill would stare:                    10
The blood that warms an English yeoman,
    The thoughts that hurt him, they were there.

There, like the wind through woods in riot,
    Through him the gale of life blew high;
The tree of man was never quiet:                          15
    Then 'twas the Roman, now 'tis I.

---

°**Title:** The places named in the poem are all in Shropshire, England. Uricon was an old Roman town where Wenlock now stands. The Wrekin is a wooded hill near the town; Wenlock Edge is a ridge nearby, and the Severn is a river.
°**holt:** a small woods on a steep slope.    °**hanger:** essentially the same thing.

The gale, it plies the saplings double,
   It blows so hard, 'twill soon be gone:
Today the Roman and his trouble
   Are ashes under Uricon.              20


## 1887°

### A. E. HOUSMAN (1859–1936)

From Clee° to heaven the beacon° burns,
   The shires have seen it plain,
From north and south the sign returns
   And beacons burn again.

Look left, look right, the hills are bright,      5
   The dales are light between,
Because 'tis fifty years tonight
   That God has saved the Queen.°

Now, when the flame they watch not towers
   About the soil they trod,          10
Lads, we'll remember friends of ours
   Who shared the work with God.

To skies that knit their heartstrings right,
   To fields that bred them brave,
The saviors come not home tonight:     15
   Themselves they could not save.

It dawns in Asia, tombstones show
   And Shropshire names are read;

---

°**Title:** In 1887 Victoria celebrated her fiftieth year as Queen of England.
°**Clee:** town in Shropshire, a county in the west of England on the Welsh
border.
°**beacon:** Beacons were lighted up and down the land to celebrate the
Queen's anniversary.
°**God ... Queen:** See line 25.

And the Nile spills his overflow
    Beside the Severn's° dead.          20

We pledge in peace by farm and town
    The Queen they served in war,
And fire the beacons up and down
    The land they perished for.

"God save the Queen" we living sing,    25
    From height to height 'tis heard;
And with the rest your voices ring,
    Lads of the Fifty-third.°

Oh, God will save her, fear you not:
    Be you the men you've been,    30
Get you the sons your fathers got,
    And God will save the Queen.

## To a Friend Whose Work Has Come to Nothing

WILLIAM BUTLER YEATS (1865–1939)

Now all the truth is out,
Be secret and take defeat
From any brazen throat,
For how can you compete,
Being honor bred, with one    5
Who, were it proved he lies,
Were neither shamed in his own
Nor in his neighbors' eyes?
Bred to a harder thing
Than Triumph, turn away,    10
And like a laughing string
Whereon mad fingers play
Amid a place of stone,

°**Severn:** Shropshire river.   °**Fifty-third:** Shropshire regiment.

Be secret and exult,
Because of all things known                    15
That is most difficult.


## The Wild Swans at Coole°

WILLIAM BUTLER YEATS (1865–1939)

The trees are in their autumn beauty,
The woodland paths are dry,
Under the October twilight the water
Mirrors a still sky;
Upon the brimming water among the stones          5
Are nine-and-fifty swans.

The nineteenth autumn has come upon me
Since I first made my count;
I saw, before I had well finished,
All suddenly mount                                10
And scatter wheeling in great broken rings
Upon their clamorous wings.

I have looked upon those brilliant creatures,
And now my heart is sore.
All's changed since I, hearing at twilight,       15
The first time on this shore,
The bell-beat of their wings above my head,
Trod with a lighter tread.

Unwearied still, lover by lover,
They paddle in the cold                           20
Companionable streams or climb the air;
Their hearts have not grown old;
Passion or conquest, wander where they will,
Attend upon them still.

---

°**Title:** Coole, in Galway, Ireland, was the home of Yeats's friend, Lady
Gregory; he spent many summers and early falls there (see line 7).

But now they drift on the still water                        25
Mysterious, beautiful;
Among what rushes will they build,
By what lake's edge or pool
Delight men's eyes when I awake some day
To find they have flown away?                                30


### Vacillation
#### IV
WILLIAM BUTLER YEATS (1865–1939)

My fiftieth year had come and gone,
I sat, a solitary man,
In a crowded London shop,
An open book and empty cup
On the marble table-top.                                     5
While on the shop and street I gazed
My body of a sudden blazed;
And twenty minutes more or less
It seemed, so great my happiness,
That I was blessèd and could bless.                          10


### Acquainted with the Night
ROBERT FROST (1874–1963)

I have been one acquainted with the night.
I have walked out in rain—and back in rain.
I have outwalked the furthest city light.

I have looked down the saddest city lane.
I have passed by the watchman on his beat                    5
And dropped my eyes, unwilling to explain.

I have stood still and stopped the sound of feet
When far away an interrupted cry
Came over houses from another street,

But not to call me back or say good-bye;                    10
And further still at an unearthly height,
One luminary clock against the sky

Proclaimed the time was neither wrong nor right.
I have been one acquainted with the night.

## Desert Places

ROBERT FROST (1874–1963)

Snow falling and night falling fast oh fast
In a field I looked into going past,
And the ground almost covered smooth in snow,
But a few weeds and stubble showing last.

The woods around it have it—it is theirs.               5
All animals are smothered in their lairs.
I am too absent-spirited to count;
The loneliness includes me unawares.

And lonely as it is that loneliness
Will be more lonely ere it will be less—                10
A blanker whiteness of benighted snow
With no expression, nothing to express.

They cannot scare me with their empty spaces
Between stars—on stars where no human race is.
I have it in me so much nearer home                     15
To scare myself with my own desert places.

## Preludes

T. S. ELIOT (1888–1965)

### I

The winter evening settles down
With smell of steaks in passageways.

Six o'clock.
The burnt-out ends of smoky days.
And now a gusty shower wraps
The grimy scraps
Of withered leaves about your feet
And newspapers from vacant lots;
The showers beat
On broken blinds and chimney pots,
And at the corner of the street
A lonely cab-horse steams and stamps.
And then the lighting of the lamps.

## II

The morning comes to consciousness
Of faint stale smells of beer
From the sawdust-trampled street
With all its muddy feet that press
To early coffee-stands.
With the other masquerades
That time resumes,
One thinks of all the hands
That are raising dingy shades
In a thousand furnished rooms.

## III

You tossed a blanket from the bed,
You lay upon your back, and waited;
You dozed, and watched the night revealing
The thousand sordid images
Of which your soul was constituted;
They flickered against the ceiling.
And when all the world came back
And the light crept up between the shutters
And you heard the sparrows in the gutters,
You had such a vision of the street
As the street hardly understands;

Sitting along the bed's edge, where                          35
You curled the papers from your hair,
Or clasped the yellow soles of feet
In the palms of both soiled hands.

## IV

His soul stretched tight across the skies
That fade behind a city block,                               40
Or trampled by insistent feet
At four and five and six o'clock;
And short square fingers stuffing pipes,
And evening newspapers, and eyes
Assured of certain certainties,                              45
The conscience of a blackened street
Impatient to assume the world.

I am moved by fancies that are curled
Around these images, and cling:
The notion of some infinitely gentle                         50
Infinitely suffering thing.

Wipe your hand across your mouth, and laugh;
The worlds revolve like ancient women
Gathering fuel in vacant lots.

## The End of the World

ARCHIBALD MACLEISH (1892–      )

Quite unexpectedly, as Vasserot
The armless ambidextrian was lighting
A match between his great and second toe,
And Ralph the lion was engaged in biting
The neck of Madame Sossman while the drum         5
Pointed, and Teeny was about to cough
In waltz-time swinging Jocko by the thumb—
Quite unexpectedly the top blew off:

And there, there overhead, there, there hung over
Those thousands of white faces, those dazed eyes,       10
There in the starless dark the poise, the hover,
There with vast wings across the cancelled skies,
There in the sudden blackness the black pall
Of nothing, nothing, nothing—nothing at all.


### Anyone Lived in a Pretty How Town

E. E. CUMMINGS (1894–1962)

anyone lived in a pretty how town
(with up so floating many bells down)
spring summer autumn winter
he sang his didn't he danced his did.

Women and men (both little and small)       5
cared for anyone not at all
they sowed their isn't they reaped their same
sun moon stars rain

children guessed (but only a few
and down they forgot as up they grew       10
autumn winter spring summer)
that noone loved him more by more

when by now and tree by leaf
she laughed his joy she cried his grief
bird by snow and stir by still       15
anyone's any was all to her

someones married their everyones
laughed their cryings and did their dance
(sleep wake hope and then) they
said their nevers they slept their dream       20

stars rain sun moon
(and only the snow can begin to explain
how children are apt to forget to remember
with up so floating many bells down)

one day anyone died i guess                                    25
(and noone stooped to kiss his face)
busy folk buried them side by side
little by little and was by was

all by all and deep by deep
and more by more they dream their sleep         30
noone and anyone earth by april
wish by spirit and if by yes.

Women and men (both dong and ding)
summer autumn winter spring
reaped their sowing and went their came         35
sun moon stars rain

## Arms and the Boy°
### WILFRED OWEN (1893–1918)

Let the boy try° along this bayonet-blade
How cold steel is, and keen with hunger of blood;
Blue with all malice, like a madman's flash;
And thinly drawn with famishing for flesh.

Lend him to stroke these blind, blunt bullet-heads         5
Which long to nuzzle in the hearts of lads,
Or give him cartridges of fine zinc teeth,
Sharp with the sharpness of grief and death.

---

°**Title:** There is ironic reference here to the opening words of Virgil's great
epic, the *Aeneid:* "Arms and the man I sing."
°**try:** prove by feeling.

For his teeth seem for laughing round an apple.
There lurk no claws behind his fingers supple;      10
And God will grow no talons at his heels,
Nor antlers through the thickness of his curls.

## Before Disaster

YVOR WINTERS (1900–    )

Evening traffic homeward burns,
Swift and even on the turns,
Drifting weight in triple rows,
Fixed relation and repose.
This one edges out and by,      5
Inch by inch with steady eye.
But should error be increased,
Mass and moment are released;
Matter loosens, flooding blind,
Levels driver to its kind.      10

     Ranks of nations thus descend,
Watchful to a stormy end.
By a moment's calm beguiled,
I have got a wife and child.
Fool and scoundrel guide the State.      15
Peace is whore to Greed and Hate.
Nowhere may I turn to flee:
Action is security.
Treading change with savage heel,
We must live or die by steel.      20

## Only the Polished Skeleton

COUNTEE CULLEN (1903–1946)

The heart has need of some deceit
     To make its pistons rise and fall;

For less than this it would not beat,
    Nor flush the sluggish vein at all.

With subterfuge and fraud the mind
    Must fend and parry thrust for thrust,
With logic brutal and unkind
    Beat off the onslaughts of the dust.

Only the polished skeleton,
    Of flesh relieved and pauperized,
Can rest at ease and think upon
    The worth of all it so despised.

### The Fury of Aerial Bombardment
RICHARD EBERHART (1904–    )

You would think the fury of aerial bombardment
Would rouse God to relent; the infinite spaces
Are still silent. He looks on shock-pried faces.
History, even, does not know what is meant.

You would feel that after so many centuries        5
God would give man to repent; yet he can kill
As Cain could, but with multitudinous will,
No farther advanced than in his ancient furies.°

Was man made stupid to see his own stupidity?
Is God by definition indifferent, beyond us all?    10
Is the eternal truth man's fighting soul
Wherein the Beast° ravens° in its own avidity?°

Of Van Wettering I speak, and Averill,
Names on a list, whose faces I do not recall

---

°**furies:** the avenging spirits of classical mythology.
°**Beast:** reference to Revelations 13:18, which applies the term to any vicious
  ruler or warrior.
°**ravens:** greedily eats.    °**avidity:** uncontrollable greed.

But they are gone to early death, who late in school                    15
Distinguished the belt feed lever from the belt holding pawl.°

## Musée des Beaux Arts

### W. H. AUDEN (1907–     )

About suffering they were never wrong,
The Old Masters:° how well they understood
Its human position; how it takes place
While someone else is eating or opening a window or just walking
    dully along;
How, when the aged are reverently, passionately waiting            5
For the miraculous birth, there always must be
Children who did not specially want it to happen, skating
On a pond at the edge of the wood:
They never forgot
That even the dreadful martyrdom must run its course             10
Anyhow in a corner, some untidy spot
Where the dogs go on with their doggy life and the torturer's
    horse
Scratches its innocent behind on a tree.

In Brueghel's *Icarus,*° for instance: how everything turns away
Quite leisurely from the disaster; the ploughman may            15
Have heard the splash, the forsaken cry,
But for him it was not an important failure; the sun shone
As it had to on the white legs disappearing into the green
Water; and the expensive delicate ship that must have seen
Something amazing, a boy falling out of the sky,                20
Had somewhere to get to and sailed calmly on.

---

  °belt ... pawl:  machine-gun parts.
  °Old Masters: great painters of the sixteenth and seventeenth centuries.
  °Icarus: "The Fall of Icarus," by the sixteenth-century Flemish painter,
  Pieter Brueghel, one of the Old Masters.

## *Conquistador*

A. D. HOPE (1907–      )

I sing of the decline of Henry Clay
Who loved a white girl of uncommon size.
Although a small man in a little way,
He had in him some seed of enterprise.

Each day he caught the seven-thirty train                          5
To work, watered his garden after tea,
Took an umbrella if it looked like rain
And was remarkably like you or me.

He had his hair cut once a fortnight, tried
Not to forget the birthday of his wife,                           10
And might have lived unnoticed till he died
Had not ambition entered Henry's life.

He met her in the lounge of an hotel
—A most unusual place for him to go—
But there he was and there she was as well,                       15
Sitting alone. He ordered beers for two.

She was so large a girl that when they came
He gave the waiter twice the usual tip.
She smiled without surprise, told him her name,
And as the name trembled on Henry's lip,                          20

His parched soul, swelling like a desert root,
Broke out its delicate dream upon the air;
The mountains shook with earthquake under foot;
An angel seized him suddenly by the hair;

The sky was shrill with peril as he passed;                       25
A hurricane crushed his senses with its din;

The wildlife crackled up his reeling mast;
The trumpet of a maelstrom sucked him in;

The desert shrivelled and burnt off his feet;
His bones and buttons an enormous snake                    30
Vomited up; still in the shimmering heat
The pygmies showed him their forbidden lake

And then transfixed him with their poison darts;
He married six black virgins in a bunch,
Who, when they had drawn out his manly parts,             35
Stewed him and ate him lovingly for lunch.

Adventure opened wide its grisly jaws;
Henry looked in and knew the Hero's doom.
The huge white girl drank on without a pause
And, just at closing time, she asked him home.            40

The tram they took was full of Roaring Boys
Announcing the world's ruin and Judgment Day;
The sky blared with its grand orchestral voice
The Götterdämmerung of Henry Clay.

But in her quiet room they were alone.                    45
There, towering over Henry by a head,
She stood and took her clothes off one by one,
And then she stretched herself upon the bed.

Her bulk of beauty, her stupendous grace
Challenged the lion heart in his puny dust.               50
Proudly his Moment looked him in the face:
He rose to meet it as a hero must;

Climbed the white mountain of unravished snow,
Planted his tiny flag upon the peak.

The smooth drifts, scarcely breathing, lay below.        55
She did not take the trouble to smile or speak.

And afterwards, it may have been in play,
The enormous girl rolled over and squashed him flat;
And, as she could not send him home that way,
Used him thereafter as a bedside mat.        60

Speaking at large, I will say this of her:
She did not spare expense to make him nice.
Tanned on both sides and neatly edged with fur,
The job would have been cheap at any price.

And when, in winter, getting out of bed,        65
Her large soft feet pressed warmly on the skin,
The two glass eyes would sparkle in his head,
The jaws extend their papier-mâché grin.

Good people, for the soul of Henry Clay
Offer your prayers, and view his destiny!        70
He was the Hero of our Time. He may
With any luck, one day, be you or me.


## An Elementary School Classroom in a Slum
### STEPHEN SPENDER (1909–        )

Far far from gusty waves these children's faces.
Like rootless weeds the torn hair round their paleness.
The tall girl with her weighed-down head. The paper-
Seeming boy with rat's eyes. The stunted unlucky heir
Of twisted bones, reciting a father's gnarled disease,        5
His lesson from his desk. At back of the dim class
One unnoted, mild and young: his eyes live in a dream
Of squirrels' game, in tree room, other than this.

On sour cream walls, donations. Shakespeare's head
Cloudless at dawn, civilized dome riding all cities.                          10
Belled, flowery, Tyrolese valley. Open-handed map
Awarding the world its world. And yet, for these
Children, these windows, not this world, are world,
Where all their future's painted with a fog,
A narrow street sealed in with a lead sky,                                    15
Far far from rivers, capes, and stars of words.

Surely Shakespeare is wicked, the map a bad example
With ship and sun and love tempting them to steal—
For lives that slyly turn in their cramped holes
From fog to endless night? On their slag heap, these children     20
Wear skins peeped through by bones, and spectacles of steel
With mended glass, like bottle bits in slag.
Tyrol is wicked; map's promising a fable:
All of their time and space are foggy slum,
So blot their maps with slums as big as doom.                              25

Unless, governor, teacher, inspector, visitor,
This map becomes their window and these windows
That open on their lives like crouching tombs
Break, O break open, till they break the town
And show the children to the fields and all their world           30
Azure on their sands, to let their tongues
Run naked into books, the white and green leaves open
The history theirs whose language is the sun.


## To My Mother

GEORGE BARKER (1913–     )

Most near, most dear, most loved and most far,
Under the window where I often found her
Sitting as huge as Asia, seismic with laughter,
Gin and chicken helpless in her Irish hand,

Irresistible as Rabelais,° but most tender for                          5
The lame dogs and hurt birds that surround her,—
She is a procession no one can follow after
But be like a little dog following a brass band.

She will not glance up at the bomber, or condescend
To drop her gin and scuttle to a cellar,                               10
But lean on the mahogany table like a mountain
Whom only faith can move, and so I send
O all my faith and all my love to tell her
That she will move from mourning into morning.


## Auto Wreck
### KARL SHAPIRO (1913–    )

Its quick soft silver bell beating, beating,
And down the dark one ruby flare
Pulsing out red light like an artery,
The ambulance at top speed floating down
Past beacons and illuminated clocks                                     5
Wings in a heavy curve, dips down,
And brakes speed, entering the crowd.
The doors leap open, emptying light;
Stretchers are laid out, the mangled lifted
And stowed into the little hospital.                                    10
Then the bell, breaking the hush, tolls once,
And the ambulance with its terrible cargo
Rocking, slightly rocking, moves away,
As the doors, an afterthought, are closed.
We are deranged,° walking among the cops                                15
Who sweep glass and are large and composed.

---

° *Rabelais:* French Renaissance writer of an inexhaustible comic imagination.
°**deranged:** unable to function properly; mentally confused.

One is still making notes under the light.
One with a bucket douches ponds of blood
Into the street and gutter.
One hangs lanterns on the wrecks that cling,                    20
Empty husks of locusts, to iron poles.

Our throats were tight as tourniquets,
Our feet were bound with splints, but now,
Like convalescents intimate and gauche,°
We speak through sickly smiles and warn                         25
With the stubborn saw° of common sense,
The grim joke and the banal° resolution.
The traffic moves around with care,
But we remain, touching a wound
That opens to our richest horror.                               30
Already old, the question Who shall die?
Becomes unspoken Who is innocent?
For death in war is done by hands;
Suicide has cause and stillbirth, logic;
And cancer, simple as a flower, blooms.                         35
But this invites the occult° mind,
Cancels our physics° with a sneer,
And spatters all we knew of denouement°
Across the expedient and wicked stones.

## The Dirty Word

### KARL SHAPIRO (1913–    )

The dirty word hops in the cage of the mind like the Pondicherry
vulture, stomping with its heavy left claw on the sweet meat of the
brain and tearing it with its vicious beak, ripping and chopping the

---

°gauche: awkward.    °saw: a proverbial saying, like "Haste makes waste."
°banal: repeated so often as to be meaningless.    °occult: dealing with
the supernatural.    °physics: reasoning power; scientific deduction.    °de-
nouement: an outcome that is reasonable and logical.

flesh. Terrified, the small boy bears the big bird of the dirty word into the house, and grunting, puffing, carries it up the stairs to his own room in the skull. Bits of black feather cling to his clothes and his hair as he locks the staring creature in the dark closet.

All day the small boy returns to the closet to examine and feed the bird, to caress and kick the bird, that now snaps and flaps its wings savagely whenever the door is opened. How the boy trembles and delights at the sight of the white excrement of the bird! How the bird leaps and rushes against the walls of the skull, trying to escape from the zoo of the vocabulary! How wildly snaps the sweet meat of the brain in its rage.

And the bird outlives the man, being freed at the man's death-funeral by a word from the rabbi.

(But I one morning went upstairs and opened the door and entered the closet and found in the cage of my mind the great bird dead. Softly I wept it and softly removed it and softly buried the body of the bird in the hollyhock garden of the house I lived in twenty years before. And out of the worn black feathers of the wing have I made these pens to write these elegies, for I have outlived the bird, and I have murdered it in my early manhood.)

## A Refusal to Mourn the Death, by Fire, of a Child in London

DYLAN THOMAS (1914–1953)

Never° until the mankind making
Bird beast and flower
Fathering and all humbling darkness°

---

°**Never, etc.:** The sentence starting with "Never" goes to line 13: "Never
... Shall I (line 10) ... death."
°**Lines 1–3:** "Darkness" does the "making," the "fathering," and the "humbling"

Tells° with silence the last light breaking
And the still hour                                                        5
Is come of the sea tumbling in harness

And I must enter again the round
Zion° of the water bead°
And the synagogue° of the ear of corn
Shall I let pray the shadow of a sound°                                   10
Or sow my salt seed°
In the least valley of sackcloth° to mourn

The majesty and burning of the child's death.
I shall not murder
The mankind of her going with a grave truth                              15
Nor blaspheme down the stations of the breath°
With any further
Elegy° of innocence and youth.

Deep with the first dead lies London's daughter,
Robed in the long friends,°                                              20
The grains beyond age,° the dark veins of her mother°
Secret by the unmourning water
Of the riding Thames.
After the first death, there is no other.

---

°**Tells . . . corn (line 9):** reveals to me that my hour has come.
°**Zion:** holiest of places.
°**water bead:** water drop, with further suggestion of prayer bead.
°**synagogue:** a place of worship; literally, to bring together.
°**let . . . sound:** offer prayers (of mourning).
°**sow . . . seed:** shed tears (of mourning).
°**valley of sackcloth:** Sackcloth is worn as a sign of mourning; the phrase recalls the Twenty-third Psalm, a reference consistent with the multiple references to religious themes throughout the poem.
°**stations . . . breath:** reference to the Stations of the Cross, depicting the passion of Christ from trial to Crucifixion.
°**Elegy:** hymn or poem of mourning.     °**Robed . . . friends:** buried with all mankind.     °**grains . . . age:** sands of time.     °**her mother:** the earth.

## Do Not Go Gentle into That Good Night
### DYLAN THOMAS (1914–1953)

Do not go gentle into that good night,
Old age should burn and rave at close of day;
Rage, rage against the dying of the light.

Though wise men at their end know dark is right,
Because their words have forked no lightning they      5
Do not go gentle into that good night.

Good men, the last wave by, crying how bright
Their frail deeds might have danced in a green bay,
Rage, rage against the dying of the light.

Wild men who caught and sang the sun in flight,      10
And learn, too late, they grieved it on its way,
Do not go gentle into that good night.

Grave men, near death, who see with blinding sight
Blind eyes could blaze like meteors and be gay,
Rage, rage against the dying of the light.      15

And you, my father, there on the sad height,
Curse, bless, me now with your fierce tears, I pray.
Do not go gentle into that good night.
Rage, rage against the dying of the light.

## In Westminster Abbey°
### JOHN BETJEMAN (1916–      )

Let me take this other glove off
As the *vox humana*° swells,

---

°**Title:** Westminster Abbey in London is the most famous of English cathedrals; it is also the burial place of royalty, statesmen, writers, and so on. (See lines 5 and 39–40).
°***vox humana:*** literally, "human voice"; a setting of the reeds on a pipe organ that imitates the human voice.

And the beauteous fields of Eden
    Bask beneath the Abbey bells.
Here, where England's statesmen lie,        5
Listen to a lady's° cry.

Gracious Lord, oh bomb the Germans.
    Spare their women for Thy Sake,
And if that is not too easy
    We will pardon Thy Mistake.        10
But, gracious Lord, whate'er shall be,
Don't let anyone bomb me.

Keep our Empire undismembered
    Guide our Forces by Thy Hand,
Gallant blacks from far Jamaica,        15
    Honduras and Togoland;
Protect them Lord in all their fights,
And, even more, protect the whites.

Think of what our Nation stands for,
    Books from Boots'° and country lanes,        20
Free speech, free passes, class distinction,
    Democracy and proper drains.
Lord, put beneath Thy special care
One-eighty-nine Cadogan Square.°

Although dear Lord I am a sinner,        25
    I have done no major crime;
Now I'll come to Evening Service
    Whensoever I have the time.
So, Lord, reserve for me a crown,
And do not let my shares go down.°        30

---

°a lady's: the speaker's.   °Boots': a chain drug store.   °One-eighty-nine
Cadogan Square: the lady's fashionable address.   °shares . . . down:
value of her stocks decline.

I will labor for Thy Kingdom,
   Help our lads to win the war,
Send white feathers to the cowards,
   Join the Women's Army Corps,
Then wash the Steps around Thy Throne    35
In the Eternal Safety Zone.

Now I feel a little better,
   What a treat to hear Thy Word,
Where the bones of leading statesmen,
   Have so often been interred.    40
And now, dear Lord, I cannot wait
Because I have a luncheon date.


## Hunchback Girl: She Thinks of Heaven

GWENDOLYN BROOKS (1917–   )

My Father, it is surely a blue place
And straight. Right. Regular. Where I shall find
No need for scholarly nonchalance or looks
A little to the left or guards upon the
Heart to halt love that runs without crookedness    5
Along its crooked corridors. My Father,
It is a planned place, surely. Out of coils,
Unscrewed, released, no more to be marvelous,
I shall walk straightly through most proper halls
Proper myself, princess of properness.    10


## Boy at the Window

RICHARD WILBUR (1921–   )

Seeing the snowman standing all alone
In dusk and cold is more than he can bear.
The small boy weeps to hear the wind prepare
A night of gnashings and enormous moan.

His tearful sight can hardly reach to where          5
The pale-faced figure with bitumen eyes°
Returns him such a god-forsaken stare
As outcast Adam gave to Paradise.

The man of snow is, nonetheless, content,
Having no wish to go inside and die.                 10
Still, he is moved to see the youngster cry.
Though frozen water is his element,
He melts enough to drop from one soft eye
A trickle of the purest rain, a tear
For the child at the bright pane surrounded by       15
Such warmth, such light, such love, and so much fear.


### To an American Poet Just Dead
RICHARD WILBUR (1921–      )

In the *Boston Sunday Herald* just three lines
Of no-point type° for you who used to sing
The praises of imaginary wines,
And died, or so I'm told, of the real thing.

Also gone, but a lot less forgotten,                 5
Are an eminent cut-rate druggist, a lover of Giving,
A lender, and various brokers: gone from this rotten
Taxable world to a higher standard of living.

It is out in the comfy suburbs I read you are dead,
And the soupy summer is settling, full of the yawns  10
Of Sunday fathers loitering late in bed,
And the ssshh of sprays on all the little lawns.

Will the sprays weep wide for you their chaplet tears?
For you will deep-freeze units melt and mourn?

---

°**bitumen eyes:** eyes made with pieces of coal.
°**no-point type:** Printers measure the size of type in "points."

For you will Studebakers shred their gears                        15
And sound from each garage a muted horn?

They won't. In summer sunk and stupefied
The suburbs deepen in their sleep of death.
And though they sleep the sounder since you died
It's just as well that now you save your breath.                  20

## Church Going

### PHILIP LARKIN (1922–     )

Once I am sure there's nothing going on
I step inside, letting the door thud shut.
Another church: matting, seats, and stone,
And little books; sprawlings of flowers, cut
For Sunday, brownish now; some brass and stuff              5
Up at the holy end; the small neat organ;
And a tense, musty, unignorable silence,
Brewed God knows how long. Hatless, I take off
My cycle-clips in awkward reverence,

Move forward, run my hand around the font.                  10
From where I stand, the roof looks almost new—
Cleaned or restored? Someone would know: I don't.
Mounting the lectern, I peruse a few
Hectoring° large-scale verses, and pronounce
"Here endeth" much more loudly than I meant.               15
The echoes snigger briefly. Back at the door
I sign the book, donate an Irish sixpence,
Reflect the place was not worth stopping for.

Yet stop I did: in fact I often do,
And always end much at a loss like this,                    20
Wondering what to look for; wondering, too,
When churches fall completely out of use

---

°**Hectoring:** intimidating.

What we shall turn them into, if we shall keep
A few cathedrals chronically on show,
Their parchment, plate and pyx° in locked cases,                    25
And let the rest rent-free to rain and sheep.
Shall we avoid them as unlucky places?

Or, after dark, will dubious° women come
To make their children touch a particular stone;
Pick simples° for a cancer; or in some                             30
Advised night see walking a dead one?
Power of some sort or other will go on
In games, in riddles, seemingly at random;
But superstition, like belief, must die,
And what remains when disbelief has gone?                          35
Grass, weedy pavement, brambles, buttress, sky,

A shape less recognizable each week,
A purpose more obscure. I wonder who
Will be the last, the very last, to seek
This place for what it was: one of the crew                        40
That tap and jot and know what rood-lofts° were?
Some ruin-bibber,° randy° for antique,
Or Christmas-addict, counting on a whiff
Of gown-and-bands and organ pipes and myrrh?
Or will he be my representative,                                    45

Bored, uninformed, knowing the ghostly silt
Dispersed, yet tending to this cross of ground

---

°pyx: box in which the Host is carried.    °dubious: of doubtful character.
°simples: plants thought to have medicinal powers.    °crew . . . lofts:
people who are experts on the technical details of the structures and uses of
various parts of the church.    °ruin-bibber: a bibber is a person who drinks
steadily; a ruin-bibber would get his "kicks" looking at ruins.    °randy:
lustful.

Through suburb scrub because it held unspilt
So long and equably, what since is found
Only in separation—marriage, and birth,                    50
And deaths, and thoughts of these—for whom was built
This special shell? For, though I've no idea
What this accoutered° frowsty° barn is worth,
It pleases me to stand in silence here;

A serious house on serious earth it is,                    55
In whose blent° air all our compulsions meet,
Are recognized, and robed as destinies.
And that much never can be obsolete,
Since someone will forever be surprising
A hunger in himself to be more serious,                    60
And gravitating with it to this ground,
Which, he once heard, was proper to grow wise in,
If only that so many dead lie round.


## *The Colossus*

### SYLVIA PLATH (1932–1963)

I shall never get you put together entirely,
Pieced, glued, and properly jointed.
Mule-bray, pig-grunt and bawdy cackles
Proceed from your great lips.
It's worse than a barnyard.                                 5

Perhaps you consider yourself an oracle,
Mouthpiece of the dead, or of some god or other.
Thirty years now I have labored
To dredge the silt from your throat.
I am none the wiser.                                        10

---

°**accoutered:** equipped; fitted out. °**frowsty:** musty. °**blent:** blended.

Scaling little ladders with gluepots and pails of lysol
I crawl like an ant in mourning
Over the weedy acres of your brow
To mend the immense skull plates and clear
The bald, white tumuli of your eyes.                                    15

A blue sky out of the Oresteia
Arches above us. O father, all by yourself
You are pithy and historical as the Roman Forum.
I open my lunch on a hill of black cypress.
Your fluted bones and acanthine° hair are littered              20

In their old anarchy to the horizon-line.
It would take more than a lightning-stroke
To create such a ruin.
Nights, I squat in the cornucopia
Of your left ear, out of the wind,                                       25

Counting the red stars and those of plum-color.
The sun rises under the pillar of your tongue.
My hours are married to shadow.
No longer do I listen for the scrape of a keel
On the blank stones of the landing.                                    30

---

°acanthine: spiny.

# AUTHOR
## AND
# TITLE INDEX

# AUTHOR
# AND
# TITLE INDEX

**(Complete poems and significant portions of long poems only.)**